# THE COMPLETE GUIDE TO HAVANESE DOGS

David **Anderson**

224

Special thanks to Vanessa Richie
for her work on this project

LP Media Inc. Publishing

Text copyright © 2019 by LP Media Inc.

All rights reserved.

www.lpmedia.org

Publication Data

Anderson, David.

The Complete Guide to Havanese Dogs / David Anderson. ---- First edition.

Summary: "Successfully raising a Havanese dog from puppy to old age" --- Provided by publisher.

ISBN: 978-1793800602

[1. Havanese --- Non-Fiction] I. Title.

Design by Sorin Rădulescu

First paperback edition, 2019

# TABLE OF CONTENTS

# INTRODUCTION TO THE HAVANESE

The Havanese is an adorable canine that looks more like a little stuffed animal that has come to life than a dog. And that look is a perfect reflection of their personality. Since it is a dog that loves to be with people, you will not want for attention nor affection when you have one as a pet. When you are home, your dog will want to be right there with you, being petted, brushed, or played with – whatever you want to do together. Your Havanese isn't going to be particularly picky about what you do as long as you do it together. The more the merrier – so long as your dog knows everyone is present.

These dogs are quite intelligent, but they prefer to use their minds to keep you entertained, which is what makes them so popular. Watching them dance around with their hair flying around them looks both graceful and hypnotic.

Though the Havanese is believed to have descended from the Bichon Frise, the dog today is decidedly different in appearance. They are native to Cuba, which is where their name comes from – Havana. They are not the typical small dog either, because they are lovers, not yappers (unless they hear strange noises, meet strangers, or have not been trained). Because of their thicker hair, they can deal with colder weather a little better than some of the other small breeds. Their intellect makes them easy to train, often requiring less time to house-train than most small dogs.

One of the reasons that people love their Havanese is because of their fur. It actually does not shed as much as their long hair would suggest. However, they do require frequent grooming, even if you keep their hair clipped short.

They are incredibly loving, but they do require a bit more attention since they are so smart. Habits like barking can become a problem if you do not train them – however, if you do a bit of training, they don't bark that much. Given their size, training is pretty easy since they can easily sit in your lap and just enjoy petting and listening to chatter. They can be incredibly energetic as well, but it is also easy to help them work off that energy through moderate exercise. Walking with them daily and playing inside will be more than enough to make them a nearly perfect dog for any home. If you have a yard, they will romp in it just as much as a larger dog, and then be twice as tired.

The Havanese is a great pet for nearly any home, though you will need to be mindful of common health problems. Fortunately, they tend to be a relatively healthy dog. They can be a fantastic companion for any family.

# CHAPTER 1
# Silky, Sweet, Cuddlers – the Defining Characteristics

*"Although Havanese are considered a small breed and are a member of the AKC Toy Group, their personalities and temperaments are very different from most 'small' dogs. Some breeders describe their temperament as being most similar to a Golden Retriever in a tiny package."*

**Robin Madrigal**
*HavanaSilkDogs*

The Havanese is a purebred dog – the only pure breed to come out of Cuba. The little Havanese is a mix of energy, intellect, and a strong desire to be with you. They are definitely people pleasers, but they also have a lot more brains than many of the dogs that are people pleasers. They loathe being alone, and they can really lift your mood when you come home from a rough day at work. Those large eyes and soft silky hair can make you forget about your other problems. Their unmistakable appearance is part of what makes them easily recognizable, in addition to being a great comfort. They are notorious cuddlers, making them one of the best lap dogs, as long as you are willing to train them. After all, because they are an intelligent dog, you have to keep them mentally stimulated - which is easy since they want to please you!

Photo Courtesy of
Zoran Gregoric

## Descriptions and Defining Characteristics

A Havanese is fairly easy to spot because they have long, flowing hair on their short, little bodies. Their large, saucer-like eyes are another give-away and are part of the reason that so many people cannot help but stop to pet them. They look like a stuffed animal come to life, and when properly trained, they are an amazing companion.

Photo Courtesy of
Deborah M Cox

## Appearance

There are two defining characteristics of these little cuddly bundles of energy and love: their eyes and their lovely, long hair. As a member of the Bichon family, the saucer-like eyes are like two dark pools that are more than happy to follow you around the house, and they are happy to be wherever you are. Havanese do require some attention and extra care as they are prone to eye ailments. Regularly cleaning can ensure their eyes remain clean and shiny.

The Havanese coat comes in many different colors, making it diffi-cult to identify them by color alone. There are actually 25 distinct col-orings, but the main ones are tan, black, cream, golden, and different types of combinations. It is exciting to choose a Havanese – there are so many different outward appearances, and you can style their hair to make them look different no matter what their obvious colors are, giving them a completely different look and possibly a different color on the lower coat.

Under all that hair, their cute little bodies look that much more adorable, just like the other members of the Bichon family. Their front legs are a bit shorter than their back legs, which makes their stride look bouncy and playful. They also enjoy standing up on their hind legs and moving around when trained to do certain tricks. They are very sweet when they wave their front paws and their hair sways with the motions.

## Temperament

**FUN FACT**
**Super Service Dogs**

As a member of the Bichon family, you may be surprised to know that Havanese dogs are often chosen as services animal because of their sweet demeanor. Since they bark far less than other small and toy breeds, they're often selected for children who struggle with things like autism.
Havanese are also used as service animals, visiting nursing homes and veteran hospitals to comfort the residents!

Looking at a Havanese, you may think that you are dealing with the typical little dog. They aren't terribly fond of strangers, so they will often be vocal when they meet someone for the first time or when they are out for a walk. However, there is little else about the behavior of the Havanese that is common of small dogs. In the home, they are very cuddly and love to relax instead of being bossy. They tend to get along with other animals and children with whom they are familiar.

They are quite intelligent, especially for a small dog, likely because they are very much people pleasers. They love to have fun and play. This is what really helps distinguish them from many other small dog breeds. As a very fun-loving dog, they are more like Labs and Goldens, just a lot smaller so that they can sit comfortably on the couch with you once they are done playing.

# Hair – Not Fur

As one of their defining characteristics is the Havanese hair, and it is definitely hair, and not fur. You can see the difference as they run around with their hair looking more like yours than most of the other canine coats. It does mean that you will need to spend more time taking care of your dog's coat, both brushing and washing. This also means that you can do a lot more to style their hair. Havanese love the extra attention, so they aren't going to be too unhappy about many of the things you do as long as you don't pull on their hair.

*Photo Courtesy of*
*Audry Roman*

# Lively, Clever, Dependent

There are many apparent contradictions about these dogs. They are intelligent, but they are very dependent. They are small, but they don't tend to be bossy or possessive. They are very loving with their people, but wary of people they don't know (although that is fairly common of most dogs). Getting to know your little Havanese will be so much fun as you train your companion. Because they are intelligent, they can learn a lot of tricks well beyond the basic commands. Their small stature and eagerness to please makes it not only easy to train them, but it is quite enjoyable.

# CHAPTER 2
# Breed History and Characteristics

The Havanese dog breed has a unique history. They are the only canine breed to originate in Cuba, and they are a member of the Bichon family. Having evolved over centuries, they took on a different personality in North America. Considering their long hair, they can do well in both warm and some cooler climates. They are very similar to many of the other canines in the Bichon family, but their history is all their own.

## The Only Native Cuban Dog

Photo Courtesy of Beth Pitcoff

When Cuba was claimed for Spain in 1492, the Spaniards began to bring dogs over as they settled and developed the island. Bichons were a popular dog back in the 1400s and 1500s. Because of their long, silky coats, this particular dog breed had better protection from the sun without having a coat that would make them as hot as other dog breeds. Since they were isolated to a little island in the New World, the Bichons that ended up living in Cuba had a limited number of potential breeding partners. With their reduced gene pool, a new breed began to evolve on the island - a breed that took on a personality and appearance that was very different from any other members of the Bichon family.

Since they were friendly and small, they became a very popular choice among the wealthier members of Cuban society. By the 1800s, the Havanese were among the most popular breeds among aristocrats on the island. As Europeans and diplomats from other nations came and visited the aristocrats, politicians, and wealthy citizens of Cuba, they became enamored with the little dog. They were so popular that Queen Victoria had two Havanese running around her castle. Charles Dickens also had a little Havanese, which made the dog better known throughout Europe, as the queen and the writer were in entirely different social circles. This appears to have been the height of the Havanese popularity, and by the 20th century, they were declining in number and were far less common outside of Cuba.

## Close Relatives

The Bichon family includes a number of popular toy dogs:

- Bichon Frise
- Coton de Tulear
- Maltese
- Bolognese
- Havanese

The Löwchen was once thought to be a part of the family, but genetics suggest they have a history that predates the Bichon breeds.

**FUN FACT**

**"White Dog of Havana"**

Originating as the only existing native breed from Cuba, the Havanese is an extension of the officially extinct Blanquito breed! Before they disappeared, Blanquito de la Habana dogs were bred with toy poodles and Bichon varieties to create the Havanese. In English, "Blanquito de la Habana" translates to "white dog of Havana."

Bichons are known for tails that curl up, little muzzles that accentuate their large eyes (creating a triangle between the black nose and big dark eyes), drop ears that flop around their face, and long hair. Some of the breeds have curlier hair, while others have long, straight hair like the Havanese. These breeds tend to be low maintenance shedders, with a couple of the breeds being considered hypoallergenic, such as the Bichon Frise.

They have long been a favorite of nobility, aristocrats, and wealthy families because of their cute appearance and playful disposition. The fact that they aren't big shedders and do not have the typical dog smell (especially when bathed) makes them a nearly perfect lapdog.

Photo Courtesy of
Ronda Flick

# Return From Near Extinction

Following their early popularity, the Havanese began to disappear and were nearly extinct by the 1970s. Since the breed was considered to be part of the wealthy, elitist class, the Havanese did not fare well during and after the Cuban Revolution. There were few Havanese outside of Cuba, and the dog appeared to be heading toward extinction.

Photo Courtesy of Cortney Stauffer

When people began to flee Cuba around the time of the revolution, they brought 11 Havanese with them. Today, nearly every dog outside of Cuba has descended from these 11 dogs that arrived in the US around 1959. Considering how the breed has been gaining in popularity, it is surprising to see that they are relatively healthy, even though the majority of Havanese outside of Cuba are the descendants of so few breeding animals. The reason why there are so many of the breed now is that people who met the 11 Havanese refugee dogs loved the little canines. By the 1970s, they began to see a resurgence in popularity, largely thanks to just how lovable and charming the little guys were. In 1995, the American Kennel Club finally acknowledged them as a pure breed. Today, people are seeking to breed the dogs outside of Cuba with more of the dogs in Cuba to make a larger genetic pool for the canine. This should ultimately help reduce the common problems that have been caused from such a low number of ancestors.

## CHAPTER 3
# The Ideal Home

*"One thing that surprises people is the breeds proclivity for high spots. Similar to a cat, a Havanese will seek out the highest spot they can reach, and not always safely!  If you sit on a sofa or a recliner to watch TV, your pup will want to perch up on the top of the backrest.  If they find a chair or a barstool that reaches your table or kitchen counter, they will suddenly be on top of that counter."*

**Robin Madrigal**
*HavanaSilkDogs*

Because they are such small dogs, usually under 15 lbs., they can be comfortable and happy in nearly any home, regardless of the size of the home. As long as you train them not to be too vocal around strangers, they will be quiet and you won't have to worry when out walking around apartment complexes.

Keep in mind that they are both an intelligent creature and a relatively high energy one. While it isn't essential to have a large yard (though the Havanese will be more than happy to romp with you if you have one), you will need to provide moderate exercise every day to keep your dog a bit calmer. Since they don't like to upset their people, you won't have to worry about them trying to sneak food out of the kitchen as much as you would with many of the other small dog breeds. However, they really do not like to be left alone and can act out if they are left by themselves for long periods of time. If you take them for medium to longer walks before leaving them home alone, they will be too tired for the first few hours to be too upset.

## Best Environment

Havanese were able to make a comeback because of their bubbly, lovable personalities and small size. There is really no best environment for them as long as you make sure to include regular exercise in their daily routine. Since they are easy to train, they can be thought of as a nearly perfect dog, and their size means they can be happy in nearly any home.

## A Compact Canine for Any Home

Their incredibly cute little frame is one of the reasons why people love the Havanese. With the appearance of a living stuffed animal, they are low to the ground and relatively light, making them comfortable additions to your lap when you want to sit and watch TV. Averaging less than 15 lbs., they are considered a small or toy-sized dog. They are not exactly hardy, so you will need to be careful as they go zipping around the floor playing with you, especially since they aren't much taller than the lower part of an adult human's shin. Of course, that means they won't take up much space and probably won't put your legs to sleep when they cuddle up in your lap.

You can purchase a fairly small crate for both in the home and travel. Most Havanese aren't terribly frightful canines, although they are not fond of strangers. Their presence in your home is also incredibly calming to you after a long or difficult day, making them a great way of simply petting your stress away as you forget about some of the things that are bothering you. Their enthusiasm can be very contagious as well. Since they can go with you almost anywhere because of their size, it is easy to see why they have been gaining in popularity since the 1970s.

## Even No Yard Is Fine – Just Make Sure Your Havanese Gets Moderate Exercise

A Havanese will be more than happy to race around a large yard, but they can be equally content in an apartment if you make sure to take them out for several walks every day, and play with them inside if it is raining too much for a long walk. They were never really a working dog, so they are perfectly happy playing inside instead of going out for long walks. Their apprehension around strangers can also make playing inside a much more comfortable experience. Going out for a bathroom break is more than enough exercise for your dog as long as you spend a considerable amount of play time inside (although getting out for long walks at least once a day is best so that they can have a change of scenery).

Considering how intelligent they are, taking a half hour to 45 minutes to train them every day can help to make them tired, as well as being great bonding time for the two of you.

Exercise is absolutely essential for your Havanese. One reason is because of their small stature. If you over feed them, they can gain weight really fast (something that happens far too often since they are so cute), and their little legs really cannot take the excess weight. The other primary reason for moderate exercise is because they are both intelligent and relatively energetic. If you take a few minutes to watch clips of a Havanese on YouTube or other video app, you will quickly see just how active this dog is. Nearly all of the videos show the Havanese running around, the long flowing hair flowing moving hypnotically. This is not a coincidence – they have energy to spare and need to move around to make sure they stay healthy and happy.

## A Warning About Apartments and Barking

While they are not typically a vocal dog, Havanese do tend to bark more around strangers. Living in an apartment can be challenging if your Havanese can look out the window and see people walking past your building. The barking can easily get on the nerves of your neighbors. You can try to train your pet to be less vocal, but it may be best just to make sure they can't see out of windows. Of course, they will usually bark after they get outside, but that is something that most people are accustomed to hearing when outdoors.

## Floor Surfaces

Given their size and fairly slender bodies under all of that hair, you want to make sure your Havanese does not get hurt running around your home. Slippery floors, such as laminate and hardwood, can be dangerous as your dog goes dashing around trying to have fun. Because it is an excitable dog, you will need to be careful that your pup doesn't go sliding into the furniture, walls, and doors. Either place rugs or carpeting on slick floors so that your Havanese has the necessary traction to prevent sliding.

## Great With Young Children and Cats, But Stranger Wary

The Havanese tends to be fairly calm and accepting of small animals and children. They are incredibly affectionate; anyone that they are familiar with is someone they are going to love. Cats, other dogs, and small children are just fine as long as your Havanese is familiar with them.

Do make sure to have an adult close when your pet is playing with small children though. You do not want them to be too rough with the little dog. All interactions with kids and your Havanese should be monitored to make sure everyone has a good time and stays safe.

*Photo Courtesy of
Jenny Prieto*

# Ideal Life-Style

*"Because the Havanese is such a wonderful breed, many people don't realize that this dog can suffer from separation anxiety. This breed does not live well in a home where they are left home alone for many hours. They can become depressed in such a situation."*

**Julie Pollock**
*Highborn Havanese*

The Havanese is a lover, not a fighter, and their primary source of happiness is being around their pack. They are not a one-person dog and will be happy as long as they are not left alone. Loneliness is something that they can feel acutely, and it is not uncommon for them to feel separation anxiety. They will basically serve as your little shadow while you are home, making you feel well loved.

Photo Courtesy of
Marilyn Deren

# Strengths

The Havanese is an exceptionally companionable canine. Their idea of fun is hanging out with their people, even if that just means lounging around the home. They will be lazy if you let them, but that is not great for their health. They can also get a little over excited if they do not get enough exercise, making it more likely that they will run through the house. While this exuberance is cute, it is also dangerous for them.

Your Havanese will also understand your positive emotions, which is one of the reasons they are easy to train. If you are laughing and chatting with them, they will keep doing whatever they are doing because they love the positive attention. Their antics are as much to entertain you and keep you smiling as they are a pleasure to do. It is also great that this kind of positive attention works well for training as it can be easy for a Havanese to pack on pounds with frequent treats.

## Common Exercise Benefits

The benefit of having so much energy and enthusiasm is that your Havanese will want to go out walking with you, playing in the yard, or just messing around the house. You don't have to do anything particularly elaborate to help siphon off some of that energy, making them putty in your lap once the exercise is over.

The Havanese is not a working dog, so it is much easier to help them expend energy. Their size means that walks are that much more efficient, as those little legs have to move a lot faster to keep up with you. Of course, jogs are really not great for them since they do not have the stride for it.

Your Havanese can help you get into better shape, though. Even if all you can do is walk them, taking three or four walks a day can help you slim down while keeping your Havanese healthy. Since your Havanese will be a couch potato if that is your thing, the walks will really be good for both of you.

## Beware of Loneliness and Boredom

Havanese are naturally a pack animal. As a part of the Bichon family, they have descended from dogs that are accustomed to living closely with their people in a home. Being separated from you is going to be a problem as your Havanese will feel quite anxious when alone. They may not be a destructive breed, but frequent, long periods of loneliness are not healthy. They will be incredibly unhappy as well, so try to make sure your Havanese is not left alone for entire days; have another dog or other pet home with your Havanese if you have to be gone for a full working day. If you have to leave your Havanese for hours at a time, have a nice sized crate and a few sturdy toys so that they can find their own entertainment until you can trust them to be on their own outside of the crate.

## Pleasers – Plan to Train

Training may not be compulsory, but it is a very good idea. Your Havanese has brains and energy, making them an ideal dog for doing all kinds of tricks. Sure, they will be a great companion even if they only know the basics, but you are really missing out on a lot of great experiences by neglecting to spend the time to train your Havanese to do at least a few of the more entertaining tricks. On rainy days or days where it is too hot to be outside, you can keep bonding with your canine while making sure the exercise levels are not affected. You will be surprised by just how easy it is to train a Havanese because most small dogs are not known for being great with tricks.

A desire to please and play has basically been bred into the Bichon family, and this is something you can use to really bond with your Havanese companion. It's also an incredibly entertaining process. Showing off your cute little dog to friends and family can be a fantastic way of passing the time, and you really could not make your Havanese happier than by putting the pooch front and center of all that attention. They love attention, and training is something they can really enjoy.

# Managing the Hair

That luxurious hair is fantastic for many reasons, particularly that your Havanese is not much of a shedder. However, it also requires a lot more care than a fur coat does to ensure that the hair does not get matted or dirty. This was one reason that they were so popular with the members of the nobility and the aristocracy – that lovely silky hair that means there is not much of a dog smell about the home. It can be styled and changed to look very interesting. However, you are going to need to make a schedule to regularly groom your Havanese at least three times a week if you keep the hair long. If you get the hair cut shorter, you are going to need to have it cut with some frequency to keep it from requiring a lot of brushing.

Baths are also a must. Just like you have to regularly wash your hair, you will need to wash your Havanese's hair - just not daily.

# A Little Dog for Those Who Love Companionship and Training

**HELPFUL TIP**
*Allergy Relief*

If you want a dog but don't want fur all over your home, this might be the right breed for you! Since the unique Havanese has hair instead of fur, it sheds far less than many other breeds. Even so, you still need to groom them regularly to prevent matting.

Contrary to popular belief, these dogs are not hypoallergenic; however, they won't irritate your sinuses quite as much as a dog that sheds heavily.

These little darlings are very enthusiastic about doing various activities with you. They want to be with you pretty much all of the time, which does mean learning to watch where you step because they are not going to stay in a room by themselves. Wherever you go, your Havanese will go.

Unlike a lot of easy-to-train dogs that learn better with treats, you are going to be able to move from treats to positive reinforcements with words and happiness a lot faster than you may be expecting. Given their long history of living with people, they can easily understand you and what makes you happy, and that is really their focus. They want to be with you, and they know that your happiness makes for a better environment. It also means that you are more likely to give them more attention. The desire to please and be with you makes training a lot easier, and can make for a thoroughly enjoyable time as your dog learns more tricks.

# CHAPTER 4
# Finding Your Havanese

Having reached this part of the book, you are probably quite excited about finding the right Havanese for your family. After all, it is difficult to beat a small dog that just wants to have fun with you and be a part of the family. There will be some training and socialization required, but first you will need to determine what age Havanese you would like to adopt, then find the right breeder if you decide on a puppy.

## Adopting From a Breeder

As with finding any other pure breed puppy, you have to spend a considerable amount of time looking for a reputable breeder. Given the fact that most Havanese outside of Cuba are the descendants of just 11 dogs, you want to make sure this has been taken into account during the breeding process.

### Finding a Breeder

One of the most important aspects to locating your Havanese is finding a breeder who actually cares about the puppies. You want to make sure that they put as much care into getting just the right parents for the puppy and are willing to spend a considerable amount of time talking to you about the adoption process, what to expect from your canine, giving you advice even after you have the puppy at home, and a slew of other important aspects. The first task to finding the right breeder is to find someone who gives the parents and newborn puppies the attention and care that is required. You want to ensure that the breeder is putting in the necessary hours to help the puppies and to prepare them for life.

Breeders who take the time to post a lot of information and updates about the dogs are the best starting points. You have very good odds that you are going to end up on a waiting list with these breeders, but for the right breeders it is worth the wait. The right breeder is going to focus on making sure the puppies and parents are happy and healthy, which will mean your puppy will get a great start in life.

After you have scanned the different breeders, you are going to need to begin asking questions and gathering information. Be prepared to spend a considerable amount of time both on email and on the phone

Photo Courtesy of
Alyssa Pawlowski

(up to an hour by phone) for each breeder you contact. Make sure to set aside enough time to call and ask questions for each breeder you are considering. This ensures that you have a good understanding of the breeder's values and the key aspects of the dog based on what the breeder offers in terms of information. Of course, you should compare their answers against each other to make sure they are being honest and up front with you. Here are some things to consider asking each breeder to get a good feel both for the kinds of puppies they raise and for how honest and caring the breeder is.

- Ask each breeder about the required health tests and certifications they have for their puppies. These points are detailed further in the next section, so make sure to check off the available tests and certifications for each breeder. If they don't have all of the tests and certifications, you may want to remove them from consideration. Good breeders not only cover all of these points, they offer a guarantee against the most harmful genetic issues.

- Make sure that the breeder always takes care of all of the initial health requirements in the first few weeks and months, particularly shots. Puppies require certain procedures to be started before they leave their mother to ensure they are healthy. Vaccinations and de-worming typically start around six weeks after the puppies are born, then need to be continued every three weeks. By the time your puppy is old enough to come home, the puppy should be well into the procedures, or even completely through the first phases of these important health care needs.

- Ask if the puppy is required to be spayed or neutered before reaching a certain age of maturity. It is possible that you may need to sign a contract that says you will have the procedure done, which you will need to plan for it prior to getting your puppy. Typically, these procedures are done in the puppy's best interest.

- Find out if the breeder is part of a Havanese organization or group. The most notable group is the Havanese Club of America. Considering the fact that Havanese groups have only recently started to become more common, there are not that many organizations; however, the dog does have a rich history, so you can find a few out there.

- Ask about the first phases of your puppy's life, such as how the breeder plans to care for the puppy during those first few months. They should be able to provide a lot of detail, and they should do this without sounding as though they are irritated that you want to know. It will also let you know how much training you can expect to be done prior to the puppy's arrival so you can plan to take over as soon as the puppy arrives. It is possible that the breeders typically starts house training (in which case, you are very lucky if you can get on the wait list with them).

- See what kind of advice they give about raising a Havanese. They should be more than happy to help guide you in doing what is best for your dog because they will want the puppies to live happy, healthy lives even after leaving the breeder's home. You want a caring breeder who is more interested in the health of the puppies than in the money they make. Yes, you could end up paying a considerable amount of money, but you should also get recommendations, advice, and additional care after the puppy arrives at your home. Breeders who show a lot of interest in the dog's well-being and are willing to answer questions about the dog's entire life span are likely to breed puppies that are healthy.

## Health Tests and Certifications

With the unique history of the Havanese, there are a number of genetic problems. This is just part of having such a tiny genetic pool. There were only a limited number of Bichons in Cuba that evolved into the Havanese breed over time, then there were only 11 dogs that left the small island and became the ancestors of the vast majority of dogs off the island today. To properly care for your puppy, you should know which diseases to watch for and how to best care for your dog.

To start, you want to see what kinds of health problems are known to exist in the parents. The following are the health tests for the Havanese:

- Hip dysplasia evaluations (OFA evaluation)
- Elbow dysplasia clearance (OFA evaluation)
- Hypothyroidism (OFA evaluation)
- Von Willebrand Disease (OFA evaluation)
- Thrombopathia (Auburn University)
- Eye examination by someone who is a member of the ACVO Ophthalmologist (they should be registered with either the OFA or the CERF)

Photo Courtesy of Sharon Russo

There are no strict certifications, but if your breeder is part of the Havanese Club of America, it means that they are working toward a set standard to ensure the puppies and parents are in the best possible shape. Being a member of these organizations means that the breeders are obligated to meet a minimum set of requirements. If they do not meet these requirements, the breeders are not allowed to be members of the organizations. This ensures that breeders who belong to these organizations are reliable and predictable in the way they treat the puppies.

## Contracts and Guarantees

As a dog breed that neared extinction and has made a comeback from a shallow genetic pool, contracts and guarantees are not uncommon. These are meant to protect the puppies as much as they protect you.

If a breeder has a contract that must be signed, make sure that you read through it completely and are willing to meet all of the requirements prior to signing it. The contracts tend to be easy to understand and comply with, but you should be aware of all the facts before you agree to anything. Beyond putting down the money for the puppy, signing the contract says that you are serious about taking care of the puppy to the best of your ability by meeting the requirements set forth by the breeder. Since they focus on your behavior toward taking care of your dog, it is a good sign that breeders want to verify that you are serious about taking care of your puppy. The contract will likely include spaying or neutering the puppy once it matures. It may also say that the breeder will retain the registration papers of the puppy, although you can get a copy of them.

The guarantee states what health conditions that the breeder ensures for their puppies. This typically includes details of the dog's health and recommendations on the next steps of the puppy's care once it leaves the breeder's home. Guarantees may provide schedules to ensure that the health care started by the breeder is continued by the new puppy parent. In the event that a major health concern is found, the puppy will need to be returned to the breeder. The contract will also explain what is not guaranteed. The guarantee tends to be very long (sometimes longer than the contract), and you should read it thoroughly before you sign the contract. Guarantees are less common for Havanese than for many of the more common pure breeds though, so you may not find many breeders with one already in place.

## Puppy Genetics – the Parents

Given the focused lineage of Havanese outside of Cuba, the puppy's genetics should be relatively easy to track, especially for breeders who are part of the Havanese organizations. Take the time to review the complete history for both parents so that you know what to expect and watch for as your puppy grows and ages. From the personality of the parents to their habits, you want a decent understanding of how your puppy is likely to behave.

It is also important to ask the breeder specifically about the parents to get a feel for how the breeder perceives them. You will have questions about the parents once you finish reviewing the paperwork, and the breeder will be able to provide a much more detailed and emotional picture of the parents.

## Selecting Your Puppy

Choosing a Havanese puppy is very similar to selecting a puppy from any other breed. A lot of it is entirely up to you and what you want in a dog. The experience can be highly entertaining and enjoyable – and ultimately very difficult. As much fun as choosing the puppy is, you do need to be careful and serious so that you are not swayed by things that you may find bothersome later.

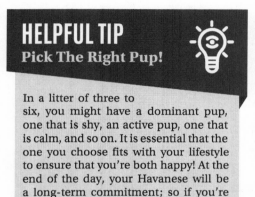

**HELPFUL TIP**

**Pick The Right Pup!**

In a litter of three to six, you might have a dominant pup, one that is shy, an active pup, one that is calm, and so on. It is essential that the one you choose fits with your lifestyle to ensure that you're both happy! At the end of the day, your Havanese will be a long-term commitment; so if you're a relaxed person, look carefully for the calmest of the litter.

As you look over the puppies, notice how well each puppy plays with the others. This is a great indicator of just how well your puppy will react to any pets you already have at home.

Also pay attention to the puppies' interactions as a pack. If you notice that most of the puppies exhibit aggressive behavior or seem mistrustful, you may not want to select a puppy from the litter. Similarly, puppies who appear to be terrified of you, such as keeping their tails tucked or shrinking away, is an indication of the kinds of issues you may encounter in the future with your puppy and training. What you want is a litter that is full of friendly puppies, even if they do not greet you immediately. Sometimes they just want to play with their siblings or figure out what is happening first.

Next, take notice if there is a puppy that is excited about meeting you. Many people take that as a sign that the puppy is the right one for their family, but that is not always true. Keep in mind that the puppy or puppies that immediately greet you are more forward and demanding than the ones who sit back and analyze the situation first.

The puppies who hang back might be afraid, or, more likely, they just want to understand the situation before they get involved. They are not the alpha types that their eager siblings are. These are the more patient and tame puppies, ones that may be easier to train.

Pick the puppy that exhibits the personality traits that you want in your dog. If you want a forward, friendly, excitable dog, the first one to greet you may be the one you seek. If you want a dog that will think things through and let others get more attention, this mellower dog may be better for your home.

# Adopting an Older Dog

If you do not want to put in all of the time and research into finding a breeder, waiting for a puppy, and then all of the necessary training, you may want to find an older Havanese. Missing a day or two of training with a puppy can pretty much put you back to square one, while a mature dog can go for a day or two between training sessions since they should already know the basics (at least housetraining). There are adult Havanese in shelters from breeders who took puppies back from people who did not meet the terms of their contracts, or from Havanese rescues.

## Benefits

There is something very satisfying about forming a bond with an adult Havanese. First, you get to skip all of the messy training that can be frustrating. Second, you get to feel like you are providing a home to a dog that really deserves it, and you can save the dog just as much as the Havanese saves you. They can be the companion you need because they are going to want to be with you all of the time. It will take a while to bond, but the dog will come with a lot less stress and frustration (or is more likely to be easier). All high energy, intelligent dogs need a lot of time and dedication to get them to be housetrained, but as long as your Havanese has already been housetrained, you can get right into the more enjoyable types of training.

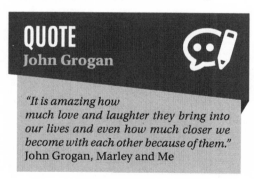

QUOTE
John Grogan

*"It is amazing how much love and laughter they bring into our lives and even how much closer we become with each other because of them."*
John Grogan, Marley and Me

It is possible that your Havanese may already know some tricks to. Exploring what they already know and starting a new training regimen is a fantastic way of bonding with your Havanese and lets them know that you are excited about spending time with them. It is an excellent way of adding them to the family.

Better still, they can help you start improving yourself. If you want to get more exercise, an older Havanese will help you get started immediately (instead of trapping you in the home trying to teach it the basics). You also have a wide range in possible activities, and your Havanese will be more than happy to join you as you explore new places or get a new look at old ones.

## Rescues

Havanese clubs have their own rescues in addition to their own breeders. You are not as likely to find this breed outside of the small clique because Havanese lovers are very adamant about how the dogs should be taken care of – and they take care of their own. The Havanese dogs that you get through the organizations and breeders have most of the necessary information that is required to sell puppies, meaning you will have the medical history and vaccination information on the dog (although if the human parent was negligent or abusive, the medical history and information may not have been tracked while the dog was with them).

There are several Havanese rescue sites that you can check out to find a purebred pet.

## Warning About Small Children and Other Pets

The potential downside to an adult Havanese is that their personalities are already established, including potential problems. If they were not socialized when they were young, there could be problems between your new canine companion and your other pets and young children. They may not be an aggressive dog by nature, but their experiences in the past will influence how they interact with your family.

Given that they tend to be wary of strangers, don't expect your new family member to be cuddly and fun from the beginning. They are going to need time to get accustomed to the new surroundings and habits of the family. It is best to introduce other pets and your younger children to them more slowly than you would a puppy.

## CHAPTER 5
# Preparing For Your Puppy

*"The Havanese has a gentle nature and are very forgiving. These two characteristics make them compatible with young children as they are not apt to hold a grudge for minor offenses."*

**Veronica Guillet**
*Renaissance Havanese*

When the day finally arrives for your puppy to come home, you and your family are likely to be incredibly excited. However, getting to that point requires an awful lot of work so that your home is ready to receive your new family member. As with any small, intelligent canine, you are going to need to do more than you would need to for puppies that are less clever. Puppy-proofing your home is a major undertaking, so you should start at least a month before your puppy arrives.

## Preparing Your Kids

Before you start getting to the puppy-proofing, you need to start by preparing your children for the new Havanese puppy, especially if they are younger. It is likely that your kids will spend more time with the newest family member because they will be home more, unless you are lucky enough to work from home. This means that they should know how to properly play with the dog – or understand that they cannot play with the canine without adult supervision. Trying to set down the rules after the puppy arrives will be a bit late because they are not going to be able to focus with such a cute puppy before them.

Well in advance of the puppy's arrival – at least a week – set down the rules and assign responsibilities. You will need to plan to review them several times before the puppy arrives too, just to make sure everyone knows what is expected of them. This includes going over the rules and roles the day the puppy arrives – before the puppy arrives.

Once the puppy makes it into your home, you will need to be present, particularly if you have younger children. You will need to monitor how they play with the puppy and make sure they are not being too rough. Make sure your children follow these five rules.

1. Be gentle. That cute little fluff ball is small and fragile. Despite being full of energy, a Havanese puppy is easy to injure, so be careful and play gently with the puppy.

   You will need to be very firm about this rule. If you see the children playing too rough or if the puppy seems uncomfortable, step in and stop the play. You don't want the puppy to be uncomfortable around your children, so you need to make sure they don't make the puppy feel trapped or in danger. If the puppy ends up nipping at this stage, it is the child's fault for scaring the puppy. Make sure your child understands nipping at this early stage is a sign that the puppy thinks that they are being too rough or scary.

2. Chase can only be played outside. The kids are going to want to run with that cute little fluff ball inside your home. Do not let them. Playing chase inside is never acceptable. From slippery floors to someone not paying attention and running into a wall or furniture, it is far too dangerous to be running in the home.

3. No playing with the puppy during meal time. Your puppy needs to feel safe when he is eating, not like he should be playing or protecting his food. If your puppy feels uncomfortable about eating, that can translate into problems later. When it is time to eat, let the puppy focus on the food without feeling like the food might be taken away or that he should be playing instead.

4. The puppy should always be on the ground. Given how cute Havanese puppies are, everyone is going to want to pick up the puppy, but this very bad for him. Explain to your children that the puppy needs to be left on the ground. If the Havanese wants to climb into someone's lap, that is fine, but no one should be picking up the puppy. Even though he is small, the puppy won't be comfortable when he is being picked up by smaller kids – and they won't be able to manage a wiggly puppy. Kids may find that the puppy wiggles too much and may not always be able to keep a firm hold on the puppy.

   This rule also applies to you too – don't pick up the puppy. With so many other great activities that you can do together, there is no need to pick up the puppy. Let him or her keep those cute little paws planted firmly on the ground and play.

5. Keep valuables and important items out of your children's reach. You may think that it is easy to keep these things away from a puppy, but all it takes is one of your children grabbing some object off of a surface and leaving it within the puppy's reach, and it is over. Kids don't tend to worry too much about what they are playing with, so anything in reach is fair game. The excitement of playing with the puppy and seeing just how that sweet little Havanese will respond to differ-

35

ent things will overwrite any thinking about what they should use for play time. If you don't want your children and puppy to destroy certain items, make sure those items are out of reach to both of them.

# Preparing Your Current Dogs

Getting the kids ready is one task, getting your current dog or dogs ready is a whole other. Once your kids start to understand the rules, you have to start helping the dogs get acclimated to the idea of a new dog as much as possible. Naturally, this requires a completely different approach. You can't set down rules and roles with a dog. However, there are things you can do to help them get ready for the newest family addition.

- Assess your dog's personality. Dogs that have not shown any problem with other dogs should be fine. Dogs that have shown aggressive or territorial tendencies will need to be monitored carefully and should never be with the puppy without an adult present. Excitable dogs will need much the same kind of attention because all of that energy can be dangerous if the dog plays with the puppy too roughly.
- Consider the encounters your dog or dogs have had with other dogs coming into their home. Any territorial tendencies will probably be something to monitor with the puppy because your dog will not understand why you are letting that puppy stay. Use extra caution when introducing the puppy. If no other dog has been in your home, it would be best to invite someone with a dog over for a play date before the puppy arrives. This will help you get an idea of what to expect. Seeing a familiar dog in the home first will help ease your dog into accepting other dogs into the territory.
- Think of times when your dog has acted protectively, either with you, a family member, or something in the home. Food is usually the most common trigger for protective behavior, but objects like toys can also make a dog feel protective.

Set up designated puppy areas and make sure that your dog or dogs cannot get into those spaces. They will need to get to know the puppy slowly over a longer period of time. Your new Havanese should not be left alone with your other dogs without supervision, no matter how much you feel you can trust them. Make sure that none of their stuff is in the puppy's area, including your dog's favorite chair or furniture. The puppy's area should be completely separate from places where your dog loves to be so that your dog does not feel like the puppy is competition for those things.

Plan for the initial meeting between the puppy and your dog to take place outside in a neutral location. Determine where that place will be before the day when your puppy will arrive, and schedule to have another adult there for the meeting. The neutral territory will ensure that your dog does not feel territorial at the first meeting. Instead of feeling a need to protect the home, your dog will be more curious about meeting the puppy, which is good. You want them to have some interaction before getting home. The additional adult is there to help. Trying to deal with an excited dog and a hyper puppy will be far too much for most people on their own, so share the work with another adult. The alpha of your home should be present for the event. If both humans are the alpha, make sure both humans are there for the meeting between the puppy and the dog. This will help establish the hierarchy with the puppy from the very beginning.

Plan to move slowly with your dog and the puppy during the introduction, especially if your dog does not have an incredibly friendly, mellow personality. It could take more than a week before the dog feels comfortable around the puppy. Considering that you are completely redoing the dynamic of your home, your dog is going to need some time to get accustomed to the change. It is understandable if your dog is not pleased too, especially if you have an older dog. It is harder on older dogs to have a puppy added to the family, and it is very likely that the frustration your dog feels will be taken out on the puppy. Make sure your dog and puppy feel safe and comfortable before leaving them together for more regular interactions.

If you have more than one dog already, all of these rules apply, but you will need an additional adult at the first meeting for each dog. Think about the personalities of each dog individually because they will all have a different reaction to the introduction of a new puppy. When it comes time for the introduction, bring one dog to the puppy at a time, not all of them at once. Your puppy will be overwhelmed and possibly terrified of so many dogs coming toward it at once. Introducing one dog at a time will help them be a bit calmer too.

# Dangerous Foods

Many of the foods you eat are not safe for your dog. Most people know that dogs should not have chocolate, but there are many more foods that are not safe for your Havanese to eat. Considering size of a Havanese, it is much more dangerous for your puppy (or adult dog) to eat certain foods.

Make sure that you never leave your plate where your Havanese can get to it and you shouldn't have too much of a problem. Unlike other smart dogs, your Havanese is not likely to go out of the way to get to food, so make sure that you don't leave people food in easy to reach places and you should be safe. This does also mean that you should not leave a book bag or other bag on the floor with food in it. This is considered fair game to a dog, and any food in that bag will be calling to your Havanese to eat it. Make sure your kids know not to leave book bags on the floor so that the temptation is not there.

Here is a list of foods your Havanese should never eat:

- Apple seeds
- Chocolate
- Coffee
- Cooked bones (they can kill when they splinter in the dog's mouth or stomach)
- Corn on the cob (it is the cob that is deadly to dogs; corn off the cob is fine, but you need to make sure that your Havanese cannot reach any corn that is still on the cob)
- Grapes/raisins
- Macadamia nuts
- Onions and chives
- Peaches, persimmons, and plums
- Tobacco (your Havanese will not know that it is not a food and may eat it if left out)
- Xylitol (a sugar substitute in candies and baked goods)
- Yeast

Those are some of the things that can kill your Havanese. However, there are other foods that could be unhealthy. The Canine Journal has a lengthy list of foods that should be avoided, including items like alcohol and other things that people give dogs thinking it is funny. All dogs have a different metabolism, and a Havanese has a significantly different metabolism to yours, so the food you eat is really not healthy for your Havanese.

To keep your Havanese healthy, it is best to keep people food off the menu. However, dangerous foods should never be anywhere that your Havanese can find and eat them.

## Hazards to Fix

The home is full of a lot of potential dangers for puppies. Prior to the arrival of your puppy, you are going to need to spend a good bit of time preparing your home so that it is as safe as possible.

Puppy-proofing your home takes about the same amount of time as baby-proofing. Plan to start a month before the puppy arrives. The following will help you target the areas of the home that are the most dangerous.

## Kitchen and Eating Areas

Kitchens are easily the most dangerous room for your puppy. From poisonous cleaners to electrical wires, there are a lot of things you will need to safeguard before the puppy comes home. You should secure all of these areas just like you would for a child because your puppy is smart and could get into areas where you definitely do not want that Havanese to go.

Not only do you need to safe-guard these things before your puppy arrives, you are going to need to be vigilant in making sure you always put those dangerous items back in their secure areas. Leaving these things out is just inviting trouble, so get accustomed to keeping potentially dangerous items out of the reach of your puppy.

Poisons should be stored and locked in cabinets where your puppy cannot go. Child locks can help keep your puppy from digging through to get to those poisons too.

One thing that totally transforms a puppy is the trashcan. It is

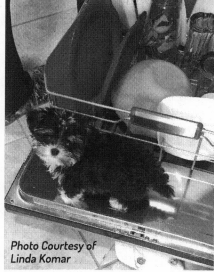

Photo Courtesy of Linda Komar

no longer just a receptacle for your food waste – it is a siren of interesting smells to a puppy. Because of the many smelly things that you throw into your kitchen trash can, you need to make sure that it is put somewhere that your puppy cannot knock it over. Whether you store it in a cabinet or in the pantry, make sure that it is out of reach of your curious puppy.

Make sure there are no electrical cords within easy reach of your puppy. This should be easy since most cords do not go close to the floor, but take the time to make sure. If there is anything that you occasionally use that has a cord that could be within reach, make sure you keep the wire off the floor. For example, if you occasionally pull out the waffle iron and its cord hangs down, get a twist tie and bundle the majority of the cord so that it won't be a problem.

## Bathroom and Laundry

The next most dangerous areas for a puppy are the bathroom and laundry room. There are poisons in both of these rooms too, so you will need to secure them or keep them well out of reach of your puppy.

Get used to keeping your toilets closed. Your Havanese may be small, but jumping is not a problem for them. Keep the toilet closed so there are no accidents. Never use automatic toilet cleaners. If you do accidentally leave the top open, you don't want your puppy drinking the poison from the automatic cleaner. This will be true for as long as you have any dogs – never have cleaner out in a potential source of water because you will occasionally forget to close the lid.

Laundry areas will be easier to prepare because they are smaller and there are fewer things that can harm a puppy. Generally, you will need to stay vigilant that you don't have dirty clothes where your puppy can get into them. Though the clothes don't tend to be dangerous, walking into your home to find dirty clothes scattered everywhere is incredibly unpleasant, especially if you have guests. There will also be times where clothing or rags will end up in the laundry that have chemicals on them. If you are in the habit of keeping them out of reach, then your puppy won't be able to get to them. You will also want to keep washing detergent, bleach, and other laundry products on a shelf that is out of reach.

The easiest solution to the laundry room is just to keep the door closed at all times. However, since there will probably be times when the door is open, make sure everything is out of reach of your puppy for those rare occasions.

## Other Rooms

Go through the rest of your home and make sure that there are no power cords in reach of your Havanese. Yes, this will be time consuming, especially near desktops and TVs because there are usually a lot of cords around them. Make sure there are no cleaning supplies out in the open. If you have a fireplace, find a new place to store cleaners and tools for it because your Havanese may be inclined to try to play with them. You also need to secure the opening from the beginning so that your puppy cannot get to it.

If you have stairs, get a gate to keep your Havanese from climbing them when unsupervised. For tables, make sure you have all sharp or potentially dangerous objects, such as scissors or sewing items, stored somewhere safe. Writing implements should also be moved somewhere safe because it is likely that your puppy will go through a phase where those items look like chew toys. You do not want to end up at the vet's office with a puppy covered in blue ink and highlighter.

## Garage

The garage is a very exciting place for a puppy, and it is incredibly dangerous. There are chemicals, sharp objects, heavy items, and a host of other dangerous items that your puppy should not be exposed to. You probably won't be able to keep your Havanese out of the garage entirely, so you will need to take the time to really clean it up. Do not let your Havanese in the garage without supervision – if possible try to keep the puppy out of the garage except when getting in the car.

All tools, equipment, and items related to car maintenance (or anything with an engine or wheels) needs to be stored somewhere with a lock. This includes objects like leaf blowers and bike tools. Your puppy is just as likely to try to chew on a bike tire as to lap up antifreeze or try to roll around in fertilizer. Keep all of these somewhere the puppy cannot go.

Fishing equipment also needs to be organized and stored in a place where your puppy cannot reach it. It can be in a closet or high on a shelf. If you store it up high, make sure there is no way to climb up to it. Do not leave any part of the equipment dangling over the side of the counter.

When you think you are done, step back and examine it from the puppy's perspective. Get down on the ground and look to see if you missed anything. If you see anything that could be attractive to a puppy, go ahead and move it where your puppy can't get it.

## Outdoors and Fencing

The puppy should not be going outside alone for a long time. There are many hazards in the yard, so you are going to need to attend to the puppy every time the puppy goes out to use the bathroom. You will need to stay with the puppy. Even if you have a fence, you will need to stay with your Havanese to make sure nothing happens.

Fortunately, puppy-proofing the yard will be relatively easy (at least compared to the inside). Plan to spend an hour or so looking it over to make sure it is ready for your puppy's arrival.

Start by inspecting the fence for issues. There should not be any breaks, holes, or loose boards. Make sure there aren't gaps at the bottom that your Havanese could slip under and get to the other side. These things will need to be fixed before your puppy arrives.

Determine where you want your Havanese to use the bathroom. Once you have a designated location, let the rest of the family know, and make sure that there are no poisons or dangerous implements in that area. Even something as seemingly innocuous as a birdbath is potentially dangerous, so make sure it is a safe place with no distractions.

Select a different section of the yard for play time. Your Havanese will learn fast, so make sure the places for playing and using the bathroom are different and your puppy learns to focus on the correct behavior in the designated areas. Give the play area the same inspection as you did the restroom area.

Take a stroll around the yard to make sure there are no chemicals or dangerous implements out where your puppy can eat them or get hurt on them. Move all of these things to a secure location where your puppy cannot get to them. If you have a shed, that is the perfect place to store them, but do make sure your puppy cannot get into it.

Make sure there are no poisonous plants in your yard. This could include gardens that have foods dogs should not eat. Your puppy is going

Photo Courtesy of Dale Hough

to try to eat things in your yard, so make sure there aren't any dangerous plants that are easy to reach.

Make sure all water areas are secured, such as pools and small ponds. Your fire ring or pit and grill need to be secure so that your puppy cannot play in them.

Walk around your yard and think of it from the perspective of a small child. This will help you identify other potential dangers that need to be addressed before the puppy arrives.

# Supplies and Tools to Purchase and Prepare

All supplies and tools should be purchased well in advance of your puppy's arrival. Even a basic list of things to get is pretty long, so start shopping for these items about a month before your puppy arrives. The following are the things you will need to get started:

- Crate
- Bed
- Leash
- Doggie bags for walks
- Collar
- Tags
- Puppy food
- Water and food bowls (sharing a water bowl is usually okay, but your puppy needs his or her own food dish if you have multiple dogs)
- Toothbrush
- Brush
- Toys

Go ahead and add anything else you would like to get to that list. Items like flea treatments will be required once your puppy gets to a certain age, so if you want to make sure you are prepared, you can get them a bit early. Starting the treatments as soon as your puppy is old enough can help protect them from a number of different ailments.

You will definitely need training supplies, as well as a training plan, particularly house training. If you want to do a mix of indoor and outdoor training (which you probably will if your puppy arrives in the winter), you should have everything you need to get started with training from Day One.

# Planning the First Year's Budget

Children are more expensive than puppies, but that does not mean that you aren't going to see a substantial increase in your expenses. Take time to budget for your puppy so that you always have the money to purchase the basic needs and maintain training. Of course, you are going to end up spending more than you plan on, so build a bit of a cushion into your budget to make sure you don't find yourself short on cash.

The best time to start your puppy budget is the day you decide to get a puppy. In all likelihood, you are going to need to spend a good bit of time researching the things you will need to do during that first year. Vets have different prices between cities and states, so you will need to find out which one has a great reputation and how much it will cost for each visit.

You probably don't realize just how expensive a puppy is. From all of the supplies you need in the beginning to the things you need to keep up the basics, dogs can be costly, even if they don't end up costing that much to feed. Starting the budget as soon as you plan to get a puppy will help you make sure you don't have any unexpected expenses.

# Keep Things Out Of Reach

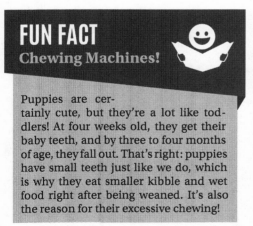

**FUN FACT**
**Chewing Machines!**

Puppies are certainly cute, but they're a lot like toddlers! At four weeks old, they get their baby teeth, and by three to four months of age, they fall out. That's right: puppies have small teeth just like we do, which is why they eat smaller kibble and wet food right after being weaned. It's also the reason for their excessive chewing!

Havanese are intelligent, which can make them a little dangerous to themselves. They don't tend to go out of their way to get into trouble, but if they are left alone for long enough periods of time, they are going to try to entertain themselves. Also, they tend to feel anxious when alone, so they may end up tearing up things that you don't want them to destroy. Keeping them in crates as puppies will help keep things safe, but it is best to simply get used to keeping all potentially dangerous, valuable, or important items out of their reach. It really isn't that hard considering the size of your Havanese, so plan for it now and you can save yourself a lot of trouble later.

# CHAPTER 6
# The First Week

When your little Havanese puppy arrives, nothing will ever be quite the same. Welcoming a Havanese into the home is like welcoming a friendly shadow into your personal space, and you are going to love it. However, there are going to be the usual puppy frustrations as well. It will be tiring and sometimes exasperating as you try to convince your puppy to do the right thing and to protect them from their own curiosity.

The first week will establish a lot about your puppy's life and the type of environment that the puppy will become acclimated to. With the puppy-proofing completed, now you get to start doing some of the fun stuff, as well as the housetraining.

## Preparation and Planning

Training begins as soon as your puppy arrives, so you need to plan for it before that day. You should have everything set up so that you aren't trying to figure things out as you go (you are going to be do quite enough of that as is, so you will want to have a baseline when you first start). Do a final check of the puppy-proofing. Given their small size, you can't be too careful about checking to make sure everything is safe for the puppy.

If you plan to keep your puppy restricted to a small area of your home, you will need to add gates to your list, as well as other items that will keep your puppy confined to that area. You will need to have everything on that list at least a few days before the puppy arrives, if not earlier. This will give you time to go out and get other items you realize you need as the time gets closer. Once your puppy arrives, you will not have time to go out and buy those items, so do as much planning beforehand as you can. Take the time to sit down with your family and talk about what is needed, especially children. They will need to do certain things, so they need to have the right tools and supplies to do them.

When it comes to caring for the puppy, you will have to be just as strict with the kids as with the puppy. The meeting with your family should include going over the rules and roles one more time so that everyone knows all of the expectations just before the puppy arrives. Training is everyone's job, but usually there is a primary trainer in any home. Responsible teenagers can take on this role, but often it will fall to an adult. You can set up

Photo Courtesy of
Sheila Burnett

pairings so that there are at least two people responsible for certain aspects of the puppy's care – such as a younger child working with you or your spouse for activities like feeding the puppy and checking the water levels. It is still primarily your responsibility, but you can let your children take the lead if they are interested in helping. It is important to make sure that the main needs of the puppy (such as feeding and walking) are covered, and the responsible party is reminded prior to the puppy's arrival.

Plan a routine for your Havanese. The plan will need to be flexible because nothing ever goes exactly as planned, but having a starting point will make things much easier. As you are working on training and regular care daily, you can start to adapt to the puppy's needs, slightly shifting the routine so that the puppy doesn't undergo a lot of changes over a short period of time – considering that puppy has already gone through a major change, it is best to keep to a routine as much as possible. Tweaking the schedule is fine, but having a schedule is essential to helping the puppy fit into the family. Once the puppy is home, there will not be time to try to establish a schedule.

That last week before your puppy arrives, make sure you have everything planned and ready. All of the planning will never be quite enough, but it is much better than trying to wing it with an intelligent puppy that may be able to use your lack of planning to his or her own canine advantage.

# The Ride Home

Training starts when your puppy becomes your responsibility, which could be before you even get in the car. Everything that your puppy should know happens during that first trip home.

The temptation to cuddle and play with the puppy will be great, so plan to be strong. You have to establish the rules so that the puppy understands them from the beginning. That Havanese brain is already working to understand the world, and it is going to pick up a lot of the world around the puppy.

Being firm and consistent will be essential for your Havanese. The first ride helps establish the family structure and pack organization.

Before picking up the puppy, ask if the little Havanese has been on a car trip before the day of the pickup. If possible, have two adults in the car for the trip home, particularly if the puppy has never been on a trip in a car. One person drives, the other comforts. Even if Havanese are not prone to being afraid of new experiences, the puppy did just leave the comfort of home and is heading somewhere in an unfamiliar environment with total strangers. That would be scary for anyone.

This is the time to start teaching your puppy about how much fun car rides can be. If you plan to crate train your puppy, have it in the vehicle and go ahead and place the puppy in it for the ride home. Make sure the crate is secure so that the little Havanese is not being moved around in the back of the vehicle. Being jostled and feeling powerless will leave the wrong impression about car rides.

# First Night Frights

That first week will be a challenge for your puppy and for you. The puppy misses home and their mother, and the new place is probably intimidating and overwhelming, no matter how welcoming you are. However, there is only so much you should do to help reassure the puppy because training has already started. If you always react immediately to negative behavior, you are training your puppy to act that way to get what they want. It is an incredibly difficult balancing act, but ultimately it is worth it. Teaching the puppy that nighttime isn't so terrifying also teaches the pup that your home is safe. If you plan to keep the puppy off the furniture, that means not letting the puppy sleep with you too, even during the early days. Once you allow a Havanese on the furniture, you cannot teach that canine that the furniture is off-limits.

*"The transition for a Havanese puppy to a new home can be diffi-cult for them and for their new owners. Havanese tend to be very vocal during this stage than at any other time in their lives. Separation times, such as bedtime or when their owners leave the home can be stressful for all involved until the puppy feels safe. I recommend a white noise ma-chine to help soothe them and placing them in an area where you can get some sleep. Sometimes that is in another room, or it can be beside your bed. Families should be flexible and try whatever works best for ev-eryone involved."*

**Veronica Guillet**
*Renaissance Havanese*

Your Havanese will probably make a good bit of noise, including fussing, whimpering, and whining. These noises let you know that the puppy is uncomfortable, afraid, or lonely. After having slept every night with mommy and siblings, this is certainly understandable. However, that does not mean you should react to the sounds.

Do not think of those noises as the problem – sure they may be a problem, but you have to learn to ignore them for now. Do not move the puppy further away from you so that you can be more comfortable because that will have a very negative effect on your puppy. The poor dear is already scared, now you are exiling it to a place where it is com-pletely alone. This will simply frighten the puppy even more, reinforcing the idea that your home is scary and unhappy. No matter how bothered you are by the noises the puppy makes, you must keep the puppy in the room with you and you should not acknowledge the noises. Over time, the puppy will be reassured that at least you are there to stay and will learn to calm down because you are present. That only works if you do not reprimand or in other way punish the puppy.

Part of being a puppy parent is accepting that you are going to have a few rough weeks with little sleep, just like with a human baby. Fortunately, puppies learn a lot faster than human babies, so you will re-turn to a more normal sleep schedule a lot faster than you would if you brought a child home.

Before your puppy arrives, you should have a designated sleep area for them, including bedding and a pen or crate. This area should also be separate from the rest of the room with boundaries that the puppy can-not escape. When your Havanese starts to make noise, you have to learn to ignore it. This will also be incredibly difficult, and it is equally neces-sary. If you give in to the whimpering, whining, and crying now, the dog will expect that to work in the future (and will get louder with each time you try to ignore it later).

Finally, you need to plan for bathroom breaks. This may be a small area within the puppy's space, or it could be a trip outside every few hours (depending on how you want to house train your Havanese). Whatever your chosen housetraining path, you will need to get up to help your puppy several times during the night.

# First Vet Visit

Always take your puppy to the vet within the first two days of arriving at your home. This ensures your puppy is healthy while creating a rapport between your canine and the vet. The initial assessment lets you know more about your puppy from the vet's perspective and gives you a chance to ask more questions that can help with any issues you have found since the puppy arrived. This trip is the baseline for which your vet will gauge your puppy's growth and development too, making it critical for your puppy's health.

The trip will definitely leave an impression on your puppy too. Odds are that your Havanese will want to explore the entire office, including the other pets. This means that you can start socializing your puppy as long as you are very careful. Make sure to ask the people who are there with their pets prior to letting your puppy say hello – you do not want the first encounter with another dog or cat to be horrifying. You want to make sure the other animals are not sick, in pain, old, skittish, or disinterested in an energetic puppy. Approach only mellow or interested pets so that your puppy has a positive encounter. The person accompanying the other pet should be able to tell you if it is alright, or warn you if a greeting will likely be unwelcome.

Remember, older animals may not feel well and certainly won't be able to keep up with the energy of a puppy. Some of them will not be up for dealing with a puppy because they are tired or have simply gotten curmudgeonly in their old age. You need to be respectful of them because someday that will be your Havanese, and you don't want them being made uncomfortable by younger dogs.

Also, make sure to give your puppy positive feedback for good behavior at the office. Being comforting and affectionate will teach your puppy that the vet's office is not a bad place (something that they will probably learn after repeat visits of "torture"). A positive environment teaches your puppy to be at ease even during a vet visit.

# The Start Of Training

Once the puppy heads home with you, the training has begun, and it won't stop as long as your little Havanese is around. You will be building on each training session for the rest of the dog's life.

This is why it is important to start minimizing behavior you don't want your puppy to exhibit.

*Photo Courtesy of*
*Ava Brown*

## Barking

Havanese are not notorious barkers, except when they are outside. This may not be much of a problem, but you still want to keep it to a minimum. Start training your Havanese in those early days to make sure barking does not become a problem, especially since they aren't prone to it. It is likely that your Havanese will start barking or making noise to get your attention, so be prepared to try to nip that in the bud, largely by ignoring the sounds if you are certain that the puppy is only angling for attention. However, if the puppy wants to go outside to use the restroom, you need to react. It will take a while for you to learn your puppy's language, so be patient.

## The Leash

Leash training is going to be about as easy as possible when it comes to training a Havanese. It will probably be more fun than expected as well, giving both you and your puppy positive bonding time. Make sure you do not drag the puppy away from things that it wants to sniff. This is how your puppy learns about the world – just accept that walks will be a long process, and plan to keep the walks short for now. Over time, you will need to learn how to get your puppy to walk with a little more purpose and a little less distraction.

## Teaching Respect

Even though the Havanese is incredibly personable and friendly, you are going to need to teach it to respect the family members. If not trained properly, it could act like a little terror. You aren't likely to have to worry about more serious problems, but you don't want your puppy to act like a brat when it gets older – that simply is not cute and gives small dogs the bad image that many of them have.

## Training to Not Shred

One of the things that Havanese hate is to be alone, and they can take their unhappiness out on items around your home. Shredding things is not entirely uncommon with the breed, so you will need to spend time training your Havanese not to tear things up, particularly when you are not around. Crate training is the best starting point, but over time you will probably want to let the puppy out while you are away too.

In the early days, it is best to be home as much as possible. Over time, you can leave the puppy out of the crate for short periods of time, such as when you walk out to get the mail. This lets your puppy know that you will be back so that it feels less panicked about being home alone.

**FUN FACT**
Beware of Puddles

Did you know that puppies aren't always able to control their bladder? Potty training can be very frustrating at times because even when your pup knows where to use the restroom, its bladder still hasn't quite fully developed. To help with this, lay out newspaper in a few selected areas of your home so your pup can get to the right place in time!

Obviously, you should keep things out of reach of your puppy, but items like paper are bound to end up getting within reach eventually. You want to make sure that your puppy understands that shredding these items is not acceptable. Be firm and consistent, but use positive reinforcement to let the puppy know when they are being good. Punishment doesn't usually work, so you will need to provide the right kind of positive reinforcement to train your puppy not to shred things at home.

## Grooming – They Don't Shed Much, But Require Considerable Brushing or Cutting

That long beautiful Havanese hair is fantastic for many reasons, including that it means your dog will not shed much. This has been one of the many reasons that the little Havanese so popular. Given the fact that most friendly dogs are notorious shedders (particularly Labs and Golden Retrievers), it is wonderful to have a dog that is relatively clean.

Though the dog is not a big shedder, their fur does require a good bit of brushing and cleaning to help it remain so gorgeous. You can always have it cut short if you don't' want to brush the puppy every day. If you opt to brush your puppy, it is fantastic bonding time. Either way, you need to plan for taking care of your puppy's hair before that puppy arrives.

# CHAPTER 7
# The First Month

*"Puppyhood can be challenging, but soak it all in as before you know it, your little puppy is all grown up! Enjoy all their fun little quirks, their bouncy playfulness, their curiosity, and their never ending love."*

**Katie Say**
*MopTop Havanese*

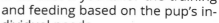

Reaching the end of that first week with your new puppy can feel like clearing a major a hurdle, and it is. However, it lets you know just how much work you are going to be doing for the next few weeks too, so you really need to pace yourself. One of the real benefits of that first week is seeing what works and what doesn't when you are training or playing with your pup. You will want to start making adjustments accordingly, because your Havanese will do best if you tailor the training and feeding based on the pup's individual needs.

*Photo Courtesy of Ana Cabral*

You will have learned by the end of that first week just what kind of energetic bundle of fur you have brought into your home. That pup may be absolutely adorable, but it can also be a lot of trouble if you don't start taking the training of your new family member very seriously. Daily practice and training will begin to show results by the end of the first month, because behind that cuddly face is a high functioning brain that just loves it when you give praise. Additionally, if you tire your little pup out, there won't be any energy left for getting into puppy trouble, so that extra time working with your Havanese has some immediate benefits as well.

# Not Up to Full Strength

Planning to train and play with a puppy is tricky. You have all of these images in your head of how you want your Havanese to behave as an adult, but the puppy simply cannot do any of those things yet. For now, the Havanese is limited not only by his attention span, but he has a lot less strength than he will have in later years. This isn't a bad thing – which you will agree with as soon as you see how quickly that cutie pie tires.

What it means is that you will need to adjust the schedule according to what your puppy can do in those early days based on their energy and strength. What appears to be boundless energy quickly shows itself to be excitement that is quickly expended by activity. Your training sessions will need to be short and incredibly basic, followed by a lot of dedicated resting (if not napping) time.

## HELPFUL TIP
### Better With You Than Without

Puppies are ready to leave their mother at eight weeks old. After the 12-week mark, or the first month of being in your home, your puppy will have developed the majority of their social skills. Your Havanese may begin to show separation anxiety when you leave the home, and cry when they're separated from you. Don't worry, it's a phase, and he'll settle down as he adjusts to your habits. The Havanese breed requires a lot of love, so you can expect to see more of this as your pup gets older.

During this time, the puppy should remain restricted to the area designated just for your new family member. Setting up a bit of space where you spend most of your time is fine, as long as the puppy realizes that these areas are where time will be spent when you are busy. It probably isn't going to take too long before your puppy feels this is acceptable because you are still present, just not available for play. If you have appropriately worn your puppy out, that will be more than enough.

By month's end, you will notice that your little Havanese is able to go for longer walks and play for longer periods of time, which will be both good and bad. Training sessions can last longer, and you will be able to start playing with your canine a bit longer. It also means that you will have to take longer walks and spend more time with your puppy. For the most part this is great, but it also means keeping up the schedule even when you feel that you are too busy or tired. Puppy comes first. At least it will be a lot of fun and you really could not ask for a more exuberant and loving companion.

# Setting the Rules and Sticking to Them

Havanese may not be quite the handful as other smart dogs, particularly breeds like German Shepherds and Corgis, but they do still have some of the same drawbacks because of their intelligence. They are going to want to see just what they can get away with, which is going to be really frustrating as time passes. Being consistent and firm with your puppy is more than enough to drive this from their minds because their biggest interest is being with you and playing. Making you happy is one of their top priorities, so if you show unhappiness or disappointment, that will go a long way to lessening any rebellion your Havanese exhibits.

While most intelligent breeds require constant reinforcement in who is alpha in the home, the unique history of the Havanese as a companion (not a working dog) is what makes it so easy to get them to behave. That said, if you are not consistent and firm, they are not going to take you or the training seriously. They need you to be consistent – no exceptions – for most of the first year or two of their lives. They may not act out the way other dogs do when a person fails to be consistent or firm, but they will look for ways to get you to make an exception the rule if it has a very desirable effect for the Havanese. You have to learn to say no to your puppy and mean it. If you don't, your adult Havanese is going to walk all over you, and you won't be equipped to say no. The cuteness difference between a Havanese puppy and an adult Havanese is not a lot, mostly just slightly bigger, so you must learn to say no to that face now – it is not going to get easier over time.

# Early Socialization

Getting your Havanese socialized during the puppy years is very important, both with other dogs and humans. They aren't exactly shy, but they are not big fans of strangers. Havanese are not unfriendly dogs; they just need time to learn to trust a new person, which can make them good little alarms in your home. However, you don't want them to bark at every person or dog you pass while the two of you are out walking, either. Early socialization will teach them that strangers are typically fine as long as they are left alone.

Havanese are not prone to little dog syndrome, so once they warm up to someone, they will be happy to see that person and to play as much as you will allow. Early socialization not only helps keep barking when you are outside to a minimum, it will make your dog a lot more comfortable and happier with the world outside of the home. Ensuring your puppy is not afraid of the world is important to making sure your puppy can enjoy life both inside and outside the home.

# Treats and Rewards Vs. Punishments

Firm does not mean that you should be mean or angry when you enforce rules. Quite the contrary, discipline teaches your Havanese to fear you instead of the things that you want the dog to learn. Treats and rewards are a much more effective training tool than punishment for nearly every dog, especially dogs in the Bichon family.

These dogs are pleasers, not workers. They get a lot of pleasure out of seeing you happy and enjoy the time you spend together. In the early days, treats will be great to get them to understand commands. Given their diminutive stature though, you are going to want to switch to other types of rewards as quickly as possible. Fortunately, positive reinforcement, such as extra petting or extending play time, is incredibly effective early in the process because of the strong desire Havanese have to see people happy.

Plan to move away from giving treats by the end of the first month – maybe not entirely, but you should be at least reducing how much food you give your Havanese for doing what you say. Work on creating a reward system based on positive attention instead. Your Havanese will respond well to this once it clicks in the dog's mind that the positive attention is associated with the desired behavior. It is far too easy for a Havanese to gain weight – they should not more than 15 lbs. (and even that is a bit too much). Treats should be ceased as early as possible to keep your Havanese healthy.

If you have to use punishment, the best thing you can do for very undesirable behavior is to deny the puppy access to you. If your puppy takes to shredding stuff up and you catch the puppy in the act, crating the puppy for 15 minutes or so will let the puppy know that this behavior is not acceptable. You do have to actually catch the puppy in the act, though. They do not understand what triggered the punishment if the misbehavior happened in the past. Those scraps on the floor have been there for minutes, so the correlation is a lot tougher for the puppy to understand. The best thing to do is make sure that there is nothing that the puppy can shred.

# Exercise – Encouraging Staying Active

*"Havanese are curious and social. They love to go for walks. While each puppy will vary in personality, they are not hyper dogs and are satisfied with a small amount of exercise daily. Teach your Havanese puppy to play fetch. They love doing this and it provides a great exercise on days you may not have time to go for a walk."*

**Carol King**
*KingsKids Havanese*

Photo Courtesy of
Laura Cristello

Your dog's small stature will mean that you have to make sure your puppy gets plenty of activity over the course of each day. During that first month, long walks are still out of the question. This is when it becomes a real balancing act determining how long to keep your puppy active. The stamina will have increased by the month's end, but it certainly is nowhere near what will be possible when the puppy becomes an adult.

The best way to keep Havanese active during the day is through regular and progressively longer bouts of training. They will love the extra attention you give them as the sessions lengthen, and they will continue to be completely wiped out when finished. That small stature means that you won't have to put as much energy in the activities as the puppy does. Those tiny little legs require a lot more movement to go a distance equivalent to your own. Use this to your favor. You can throw toys short distances and have the puppy bounce after it in the yard. You can take walks to different areas in an effort to gauge just how much stamina your puppy has each week. Do keep in mind that you should not be picking the puppy up even on a walk, so keep it an easy walk home for when your puppy tires so they can walk home too.

Pay attention to what your puppy really enjoys and include that in regular activities.

# Best Activities

This one is really up to your Havanese. Some of them adore training, some love walks, and others just want to play. While you should be engaging in all three of these activities, your Havanese will show what activities are best for them at this stage and for their individual personality.

Playing is easily the quickest way to tire your puppy. Basic games like tug-of-war and chase use up a lot of energy and are great for bonding. However, they don't really teach your Havanese much. Use play time to burn off extra energy or after a training session if your puppy seems to still have energy to spare.

Walks are great because of the change in environment. For all intelligent dogs, exploration is a great activity. As long as you are on the walk too, your puppy is going to be very excited about going to new places. The thing to be wary of is how your Havanese reacts to strangers. Havanese are particularly wary of strangers, which could be problematic given how adorable they are. Socialization is going to be extremely important to keep your Havanese from being a barking nuisance every time you walk past someone new. Taking walks in those early days will definitely help to fight that tendency.

Photo Courtesy of
Kim Davis

Training is the best way to keep your Havanese active and learning. It creates a fantastic bond between you and the puppy, and it gives you a chance to see just how quickly they can learn.

# CHAPTER 8
# Housetraining

Photo Courtesy of Karen Rose

Housetraining is the least favorite task for any puppy parent, but it is essential for both a healthy adult canine and a clean home. It is tedious training and there will be days where you will feel like the training isn't going well, but you need to keep pressing on all the same. At least with a Havanese, it should be a somewhat easier task because your dog wants you to be happy. Being an intelligent canine, they are going to realize that their habit of using the bathroom in the wrong place makes you unhappy and will want to change that. Before you start the training, you need to implement these two rules:

1. Havanese puppies should not be free to roam when no one is present. They need to be monitored when they are out of their designated puppy area. Your Havanese is not going to want to be in a soiled crate, so there is a much lower risk of your puppy having an accident in the crate or their small puppy area.

2. Your puppy should have constant, easy access to the location where you plan to do the training. Alternatively, you must be prepared for frequent outdoor trips once you start housetraining.

When these rules are established and understood among all family members (everyone will need to help enforce them), you have to make a few decisions about the training itself.

## Understanding Your Dog

Havanese are intelligent but very dependent dogs. Their desire to please their people is what helps them to quickly understand what it is you are trying to train them to do. Once they understand what you want, they are going to start trying to do that regularly, as long as you are consistent with the training. However, that does not mean that your puppy is going to be housetrained within a week. It is going to take as long to train your Havanese as it takes with most other intelligent dogs (well, maybe a little less time, but no guarantees).

If you are inconsistent, your Havanese is not going to be easy to train. They need to know that the rules always apply to understand that they must regularly use a puppy pad or the outdoors to do their business. If you decide to train in the home with a puppy pad, be aware that you will need to quickly move the training outside. It will be difficult for the puppy to understand why it is suddenly not acceptable to use the bathroom inside – or to understand where the puppy pad has gone. If possible, plan to train your Havanese to go outside from the beginning unless it is winter and too cold for your puppy to focus.

Havanese do prefer a clean space, so they will be glad to know where they should be doing their business. They will also be pleased to know that the mess will be cleaned up so that they aren't going to have to walk through it later.

# Inside or Outside

While you should have your Havanese using the bathroom outside as soon as possible, you may need to start with indoor training, particularly if it is a cold winter when your puppy arrives. If you do begin inside, you need to quickly train your Havanese that the only place where it is acceptable to use the bathroom is in the designated space.

If you start with outdoor training, be prepared to take your puppy out a lot, even at night when you would prefer to be sleeping. This is a very frustrating, tiring, and time-consuming job, but fortunately this is only for a short period of time given how quickly your Havanese will learn if you are dedicated to housetraining your puppy.

Sticking with outdoor training will make housebreaking easier in the long run. You will need to have a designated space picked out before your puppy arrives, and you will need to stick to it. Keeping the designated area close to the door will make it an easier task since your puppy will be able to quickly get to the spot after walking outside. If you have an area picked out where you want your puppy to go, it will be easier to teach this from the beginning. Then you won't have to spend lots of time cleaning up your yard every week (at least not for the waste of your

Photo Courtesy of Sara Mullen

Havanese). If you want to do this, you need to make sure to train him from the beginning, otherwise your Havanese is not likely to listen to you when you try to shrink the space it has for using the bathroom.

Leash training can make it easier to keep your puppy focused when you go out to use the bathroom. It also ensures your puppy goes to the designated spot in the early days.

# Establish Who Is Boss – Kind But Firm

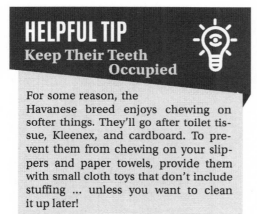

**HELPFUL TIP**
**Keep Their Teeth Occupied**

For some reason, the Havanese breed enjoys chewing on softer things. They'll go after toilet tissue, Kleenex, and cardboard. To prevent them from chewing on your slippers and paper towels, provide them with small cloth toys that don't include stuffing ... unless you want to clean it up later!

Being consistent and firm is the key to training every dog, especially one as loving and sweet as a Havanese. There are going to be times when you want to say that something is close enough, especially when those large eyes beg you to head back inside. Don't give in. If you do, then your Havanese is going to know how to get you to relent again. Training is all on you and your ability to stick to the rules that you set.

Regular bathroom break intervals are the best way to make sure that this is not a problem. When your puppy is able to anticipate a bathroom break, waiting will be easier so that they can follow your rules.

# Positive Reinforcement – It's About Respect

Despite being incredibly personable, the Havanese will need to learn to respect you, not just enjoy your company. Once your puppy learns you are the boss and respects your rules, positive reinforcement will be all your puppy needs to follow the rules of using the bathroom outside.

Your Havanese wants to do things your way, which is what makes the training so easy. Positive reinforcement will quickly become the best reward you can offer your puppy to do the right thing and go outside. The desire to have a clean space will help as well. This is why it makes it easy for you and your family to train the newest member.

It is not effective to punish a Havanese for accidents. Odds are that you will not be there when the accident happens, so the puppy is not going to tie the punishment to the accident and will not understand why you are angry. This means that you are not teaching the lesson you want the puppy to learn; you are just teaching the puppy to fear you when you get home or in the room.

Remember, these little puppies adore having you around, and they want you to be in a good mood. This makes them easier to train than most little dogs because they react very well to positive reinforcement.

# Regular Schedule, Doggie Door, or Newspapers?

One of your final considerations is to figure out how you plan to train your Havanese puppy. Much of the answer is going to depend on where the training will begin – inside or outside of your home.

Havanese are more likely to use the bathroom after a few specific events:

- After waking up (in the morning or after a nap)
- After being in a crate for a few hours
- When on the leash

Pay attention to the behavior of your Havanese to determine when it is more likely for your puppy to need to go to the bathroom. This can help speed up the training process.

*Photo Courtesy of Crystal Singleton*

# It's All On You – Havanese Like It Clean

Havanese have a long history of living with humans and enjoying their lives. They enjoy being brushed and washed more than most dogs because it means spending time with you. They enjoy having clean spaces too, which is something you can use to make potty-training that much easier. Housetraining is completely on you because all your puppy desires is to do what you want him to do, as well as a preference for having a clean home. If a Havanese does not understand the training, it is very likely that it is something you are doing wrong with the training. Being consistent and firm while being positive and encouraging will make this particular training a lot easier than with most small dogs.

# CHAPTER 9
# Socialization and Experiences

Intelligent dogs tend to need more work when it comes to socialization. Havanese are a fantastic breed, and as long as they are socialized from an early age, they make the perfect little companion. It is unlikely that socialization will remove all of their mistrust of strangers, but they won't be as anxious around them if they are in environments with strangers regularly from a young age.

You will have to plan and dedicate time to socializing your Havanese from the day your puppy arrives. Without socialization, training is not going to go quite the way you want it to go. Your Havanese needs to feel comfortable interacting with other animals and people, which can only be done by going outside and being around others.

## Benefits Of Socialization

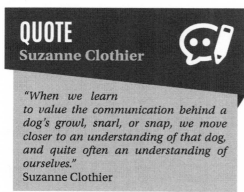

**QUOTE**
**Suzanne Clothier**

*"When we learn to value the communication behind a dog's growl, snarl, or snap, we move closer to an understanding of that dog, and quite often an understanding of ourselves."*
Suzanne Clothier

Havanese love their people, but they do take some time to warm up to people they don't know. When they are puppies, they will warm up to you and your family relatively quickly because you are constantly with them, so you won't be strangers for long. Havanese are not a naturally aggressive dogs (far from it), but they do get anxious when around unfamiliar people. As a Havanese parent, you want to make sure your canine is happy and well-adjusted.

### Problems Arising From Lack Of Socialization

One of the few problems you are likely to have with your Havanese is barking and the general unease they will feel around people they do not know. Sometimes this does extend to other dogs as well. It is possible that your Havanese will feel a greater aversion and anxiety (or just plain terror) around strangers because they are not exposed to enough diversity to know that most people are fine.

By taking them outside often early in their lives, Havanese learn not to be so afraid or defensive, which makes walking your dog much more pleasant. It may not exactly stop them from barking a lot while out of the home, but they will at least be happy or excited about the encounters instead of being anxious or afraid.

## Your Challenges With an Anxious Dog

Photo Courtesy of Melissa Telsey

Havanese are not intimidating dogs, except to little kids. Then a barking dog can be terrifying, no matter how small it is. There are also people who are afraid of dogs, and if your Havanese is not socialized from an early age, the fear of the person and the anxiousness of the dog will be a bad mix. Havanese may not be known for nipping or biting, but you never know how a dog will react in situations where both sides are extremely uncomfortable. Socialization makes it so that your canine is more excited and happier to see new people, instead of feeling anxious. Given how prone Havanese are to enjoying the company of people, this can give people who have had negative experiences with dogs a positive experience to help them overcome their current thinking about canines.

## Why Genetics Matter

Genetics are important because Havanese tend to be uncomfortable around strangers. Having doggy parents that are more comfortable around people will be passed down to their puppies, which will make their socialization easier. Knowing the temperament of the parents prior to bringing your puppy home will help you determine whether your puppy is likely to develop a personality that will work well with your family. If the parents tend to be skittish or standoffish, it is likely your puppy will be more inclined to share that temperament.

Photo Courtesy of Barbara Knight

### Natural Aversion To Strangers – A Blessing and a Curse

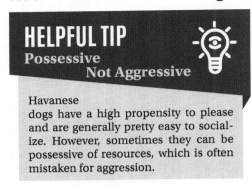

**HELPFUL TIP**

Possessive
Not Aggressive

Havanese dogs have a high propensity to please and are generally pretty easy to socialize. However, sometimes they can be possessive of resources, which is often mistaken for aggression.

Not trusting strangers can be a problem, but it can also make your little Havanese a better alarm in the home. Obviously, having a constantly barking dog when going out for a walk can be really annoying. The discomfort to both you and your Havanese will be a real nuisance, making walks very unpleasant if your canine is not socialized from an early age. While it is possible to work on it with older dogs, it is far more difficult to socialize dogs once they are no longer puppies.

On the plus side, having a Havanese that barks at strangers in and around your home is a good thing (unless they are your guests). They are not guard dogs, but they can be little alarms if someone is trying to get into your home.

# Common Problems

Barking at strangers is easily the most common problem with Havanese. Considering the fact that they should go out for walks nearly every day, you really have to make sure to socialize them so that the walks are not unpleasant experiences. By teaching them that strangers aren't so bad, you and your Havanese can enjoy those necessary walks a lot more.

A puppy with a good temperament will not experience the same kind of aversion that an adult Havanese feels, which makes socialization much easier. Given how exuberant and easygoing they are, socialization is not a difficult task as long as you make sure that they learn that being outside and meeting strangers isn't a terrifying experience.

# Properly Greeting New People

Every Havanese is different, and when they are puppies, they are naturally curious and energetic. Their reluctance and aversion to strangers will likely be present when they are young (if they are inclined to that temperament), but it is still fairly easy to overcome. To ensure your

Havanese understands how to interact with strangers, take them out to meet new people often. It can be a lot of fun, and your puppy will learn not to be afraid when going outside. People will enjoy meeting your adorable little furball too because Havanese puppies are so incredibly cute. The difficulty is finding time to reinforce the positive behaviors and teach the puppy to enjoy these encounters.

Greeting new people is typically easy when away from home since people will want to meet your puppy. It is also easy to introduce new people at home if you have friends who are willing to come visit to help socialize your puppy. Once your Havanese sees that you are comfortable around the stranger, they will naturally adapt a similar attitude toward the person. However, you will need to go out to meet new people too because your Havanese will not be spending his or her entire life inside your home. That means getting comfortable with the idea of meeting people outside.

# Behavior Around Other Dogs

Photo Courtesy of Susan Mahar

This companion dog also enjoys the company of other dogs. They don't really care so much about the hierarchy of the pack as long as they get to be with everyone. They will have a favorite person in the family, but when you aren't around, another dog or other dogs can help alleviate separation anxiety.

You will need to introduce them slowly at first because puppies can be difficult for some dogs to accept, no matter how friendly the puppy is. Havanese are incredibly agreeable dogs and don't need to be the alpha, which make them easier to integrate within the pack.

# CHAPTER 10
# Being a Puppy Parent

Playing with a Havanese puppy is a fantastic experience because they are really developing a bond with you, and all of that energy is spent getting to know you. They want to be with you all the time, even when they are sleeping. They give your world an entirely new perspective that most people will never experience. Sometimes the view is filtered through a safety lens because you want to keep your puppy safe. Other times you will see things with more awe because of how excited your little guy will get by new experiences. This part of being a puppy parent is very rewarding. However, with all of that enjoyment comes some less than desirable behavior. Virtually every puppy goes through a phase when they are difficult and destructive, and that will be both cute and frustrating.

**FUN FACT**
**The Teenage Years**

Did you know puppies officially become adults at one year old, but they aren't fully mature until they've reached two years of age? That means that as the parent of a Havanese pup, you'll need to have patience. Be calm when giving commands, and give your pet plenty of one-on-one time when you're at home to prevent destructive behaviors.

Havanese are not particularly difficult because they quickly realize that certain actions make you unhappy, which they will quickly want to avoid. Their intelligence means that they will be able to understand what is considered bad behavior earlier than many other small dogs, and unlike intelligent work dogs, they don't tend to use their brains to make mischief when your back is turned. Because they are incredibly affectionate and personable, you will be able to keep them with you most of the time. That means you will frequently be able to catch them when they are misbehaving, making it easier to let them know that certain behaviors and activities should be avoided.

When properly trained, your Havanese will be a virtually perfect companion, almost like an extension of yourself. It will take some very firm and consistent training in the early days. This is easier said than done given how adorable the Havanese puppies are.

# Staying Consistently Firm

This is going to be one of the most difficult aspects of being a puppy parent to a Havanese. With those adorable little bodies and large eyes, you are going to want to make exceptions to the rules, something that your puppy will learn how to manipulate. Yes, they want to be with you and make you happy, but if you are willing to make exceptions, their intelligence will mean they will quickly learn what endearing actions make you allow some transgressions. Considering the fact that they usually don't try to outsmart their people, it is easy to think that what they want aligns with

Photo Courtesy of
Madelyn Quance

what you want. Just because they are not headstrong does not mean that they don't enjoy doing things that they shouldn't; they just don't go out of their way to do them if they know that you mean what you say.

During that first year, you really cannot afford to make any exceptions for your Havanese puppy. They are learning what they need to know about the world from you, and if you start to make exceptions, it teaches them a lesson you really don't want them to learn. Be firm and consistent to help train your Havanese to be the ideal companion going forward. This not only makes having your Havanese more enjoyable, it means that your Havanese is likely to be healthier (since most of the exceptions tend to be food-based, and your Havanese really should not be eating people food).

Like dealing with children, Havanese need the rules to be in place all of the time and need to fully understand those rules before you start letting the puppy "get away" with breaking them.

# Puppy Gnawing and What to Watch

It is simply a universal truth – puppies gnaw on virtually anything and everything they can get their little maws on. Initially this habit forms because they are teething, and the feel of biting something makes them feel better. As they age, it is part of learning about the world and how they should interact with it. Havanese are relatively easy to train out of this bad habit, but you do need to be firm and consistent for your puppy to understand when chewing is appropriate and when it isn't.

*Photo Courtesy of Bill Shrum*

For the first few months after your puppy's arrival, your Havanese should be secured in a location with a very limited number of things to chew on. Given how small their mouths are, you would think this would be easy, but it is surprisingly difficult because they will find things you didn't even think of as being chewable. Look over the area with this in mind. If something looks like an item your puppy can chew (they don't have a point of reference about an object until they interact with it, and their mouths are typically the first interaction they will try), you need to get it out of the puppy's area.

You will also need to make sure there is no way for your puppy to escape this area. You should also ensure there is no furniture or other moveable objects that can be pushed out of the way, crawled under, or otherwise bypassed so that your adorable little bundle can get out of the designated puppy area. Since your Havanese is going to want to be with you, there is a good chance they will try to make a break for it to find you if they are left alone. Making sure they cannot get out will help keep them for chewing on things they shouldn't.

When your puppy is not in this designated area, you must keep an eye on the little darling the entire time your puppy isn't in the area. Just like when you are taking care of babies and young children, you cannot turn your back on a young puppy. If you are busy or need to focus on something else, put the puppy in the designated puppy space to ensure that your Havanese does not chew on things that are within reach (or engage in other activities that could harm them).

Having toys, particularly chew toys, will help your puppy learn that there are designated things for their mouths besides food. Keeping these toys in the designated puppy area will also give your puppy something to do while you are busy elsewhere. When it is time to play outside of the designated area, make sure to bring one or two of the toys so your puppy understands that the other items in the room are not for chewing. This helps speed up the learning process as the puppy already knows the toys are fine for chewing when he or she is in the puppy space, which easily translates to outside of the space as well.

# Barking, Barking, and More Barking

Overall, the Havanese is a fairly quiet dog that sticks to you like a shadow. However, there will be times when this wonderful companion will take to barking, and that is when your patience will be tried. Puppies are still learning about their voices, so they need to be able to express themselves. At the same time, you don't want them to become little yappers.

Barking is most likely to be a problem when you aren't home. Given the Havanese's suspicion of strangers, they are going to let strangers know that they are watching. It may also be that the puppy is excited about meeting someone new and voices that desire. It is more challenging to get a Havanese to stop barking because they aren't inclined to do it except for in a few situations (ones that you may prefer they bark). If your puppy tends to bark for attention, it is fairly easy to get that habit to stop by ignoring the puppy until silence has been established for a few seconds. Then give your puppy attention and love. Reward the quiet times and ignore the puppy during barking periods to get the point across. This is much harder to do when the two of you are outside because they are not trying to get your attention, but someone else's. This probably won't be a significant problem, so it may not require much training if you are alright with the occasional bark on a walk.

# Destructive Behavior

Destructive behavior is a concern for every puppy parent, even Havanese puppy parents. Sometimes they are simply trying to get your attention, other times they are trying to entertain themselves when you aren't around. Whatever the reason, you need to make sure that your puppy has a proper outlet for all of that energy and intellect.

## Inside

Havanese have a limited reach, but don't forget that they can also reach anything that is near furniture that you allow them on. If you let your puppy on the couch, any tables near the couch should have nothing on them, or they need to be far enough from the couch that the puppy cannot reach any of the objects on the table. If you leave writing implements, coasters, or other objects on surfaces that your puppy can reach, you should be aware that it is likely that your puppy may decide that the object is a toy.

You will need to plan ahead for training your Havanese with the following two activities:

- Training your pup not to be destructive
- Getting accustomed to keeping anything you don't want chewed on out of reach of your puppy

Chew toys are certainly a huge help, and you can keep one or two on the couch to keep your puppy from looking for things once they are allowed to be outside of their designated area. Your puppy should not be let out of the designated area when you are not home though, at least not in the early days. You should be around to make sure they don't chew on things that they shouldn't when out of their area. To keep the puppy safe, you need to keep the Havanese locked up when you are unable to focus all of your attention on the puppy for the first few months too.

## Outside

Just like when you are inside, you should keep a constant eye on your puppy when you are outside to curb any destructive tendencies. If you turn your back, your Havanese will probably try to get your attention back; but failing that, they may decide to start tearing up a garden, plants, or other items in the yard.

Do not leave your Havanese outside alone, either as a puppy or as an adult. They are not an outdoor dog and will not be happy being exiled from the family. This could manifest in your Havanese figuring out

Photo Courtesy of Mari Jordan

how to escape the backyard, hoping to find a way to get to you. Be with your puppy for the entire time the Havanese is outside to make sure the puppy is safe.

## Managing the Behavior

With all of that energy and intellect, the best preventative for destructive behavior is to be constantly attentive to your puppy when you are outside of the puppy area. Havanese are a lot of fun to be with, so it really isn't a chore or annoyance most of the time. Play time and walks will be plenty to make the puppy tired enough to behave in the early days.

Being a constant companion and a firm advocate of the rules will make your puppy a very obedient and happy dog. During the early days and months, you should spend as much time with the puppy as possible. Making sure the puppy is too tired to do anything inappropriate will go a long way to making the puppy more malleable for the behaviors you want to encourage because the puppy will be too tired to cause problems. You should also start training as early as possible so that the puppy's stamina will improve after the puppy has learned the basic rules.

# Play Time!

This is the activity you are probably looking forward to doing the most with your Havanese. They love being with you and having your undivided attention, and you will enjoy just resting and playing lackadaisically with the puppy. No to mention, these puppies are absolutely adorable, and getting to watch them play with enthusiasm is a huge stress reliever. Make play time a regular part of your daily schedule, not only to help train your puppy and establish a close bond, but to help relieve your own stress.

Havanese do not like to be left alone, and playing with them is how to make them too tired to be upset if you have to leave for a little while. They are learning the rules and boundaries at this point, so making them too tired to act out while you are busy will make it easier to praise them for behaving the way you want them to behave. Training your Havanese can be a life-long activity, but what you teach them during that first year will play a large role in how much and how well they learn later. Remember, this is the foundation for all of their training as an adult canine.

Beginning the training for tricks during this time is ideal. This helps keep them out of trouble and establishes the necessary rapport to train them in more advanced tricks later. It is also a remarkably enjoyable way to engage your Havanese in physical and mental stimulation that will reduce the tendency to chew or destroy objects in the puppy's reach.

Havanese are people pleasers. Watching them do tricks, then letting them cuddle up with you is incredibly rewarding and impresses nearly everyone who comes to visit or sees you playing together while you are at a park. Playing with your puppy in the beginning provides a safe and fun environment to learn how to behave so that you can more thoroughly enjoy your time together later. Your dedication to consistent training during that first year or two will equate to an adorable, loving, loyal life-long companion.

*Photo Courtesy of
Marilyn Deren*

# CHAPTER 11
# Living with Other Dogs

Havanese may prefer to be with people, but they will be happy to hang out with other dogs, especially when people are not around. Because they are the type of dog that hates being alone, having more than one dog in the house will make it easier for your Havanese when you aren't at home.

Since Havanese aren't particular about who is alpha, they will easily find their place in a hierarchy that will make everyone happy. Just like they only want to spend time with you, they will be happy being around other dogs.

## Introducing Your New Puppy

Photo Courtesy of
Karen Rose

Your puppy needs to meet all of your current dogs in a neutral place so that no territorial instincts create a problem. By meeting the puppy somewhere that your current dog or dogs do not think of as theirs, you will make everyone feel more at ease during the first introductions. It doesn't matter what breed the puppy is, this is always true when introducing a new dog into your home.

As your new family member and the rest of the canine pack start to get acquainted and feel comfortable with each other, you can head home. As they enter the home, they will have a bit more familiarity with each other, making your current dogs feel more comfortable with the new addition to the family. This sense of familiarity does not mean that they will be bonded, so there may be some tension, especially early on. This is why it is important to keep them separated when you aren't home. The puppy should be in the designated area, and it will be easier for your puppy to relax and start to get familiar with the new environment there. Since you set the special area up prior to your pup-

**HELPFUL TIP**

**Stranger Danger**

Since Havanese dogs are so easy to socialize, they get along easily with other pets and people in the home. However, they are wary of strangers, both canine and human, and may appear to be more timid than other breeds when introduced for the first time.

py's arrival, it will be much easier to start getting your puppy acclimated to the area.

Make sure that none of your other dog's stuff ends up in the puppy's area. This can be seen by your dog as a threat to his or her place in the pack and will generate unnecessary tension between your dog and the new puppy. The puppy will probably chew on anything and everything in the puppy's area, including things that belong to your other dog. At this stage, possession doesn't mean anything to your little Havanese. Your dog, on the other hand, will see this as a challenge, likely resulting in very negative behavior. This will be true when your puppy is out of the puppy area too. Make sure that all of your dog's stuff is out of the puppy's reach at all times. Before taking the puppy out of the designated area, make sure to do a bit of cleanup and store the dog's toys in a safe place.

Meal time is another potential problem, so your puppy should be eating in a different location, at least in the beginning. Food tends to be the source of most dog fights and unnecessary tension. As your puppy gets older, you can start to feed your Havanese with your other dogs, but keep them separated for now.

Your current dog probably isn't going to be happy about sharing you with the puppy either. Be prepared to make sure your dog knows you still care about them after the puppy arrives because your dog is going to be pretty uncertain with the new addition. Schedule one-on-one time with your older dog, including longer walks, extra training, or general play. This will let your dog know that the puppy is not a replacement. You should start keeping a schedule with your dog that you don't change after the puppy arrives. It also means you will need to be just as firm and consistent with your puppy as you are with your dog. If you are more lenient with your puppy than with your dog, this will create tension between them.

There are a number of benefits to having a dog in the home who already knows the rules. The biggest is that your dog will also start scolding your puppy for misbehavior. Since your dog isn't likely to be swayed by how cute the puppy is, your dog will have a much more objective approach to training. Of course, your dog cannot be the primary trainer, but it is nice to have someone helping reinforce the rules and showing the puppy how things are done. Having a dog to set an example helps the puppy better understand where he or she is in the pack while learning what behaviors are unacceptable. As long as your dog is gentle with the new member of the family, it is alright to let your well-behaved dog scold and reprimand your puppy – just make sure there isn't too much aggression or roughness to the behavior correction. Having your own canine babysitter also helps establish a better relationship between the canines.

Should your dog opt out of this role, that isn't a problem either. There is no need to force a role on your current dogs because their behavior will be enough to show the puppy how to behave. It is best to let your dog decide what kind of relationship to have with the puppy.

*Photo Courtesy of Donna Ward*

# Relaxed Dog Mentality

Fortunately, having a dog that has centuries of relating directly to people in the home means that you will have a much easier time integrating them into the family. Havanese want to find the most natural fit for their environments, and they aren't going to be too picky about where they are in the hierarchy as long as they get to spend the majority of the time with you. Your dog will work as a perfectly acceptable surrogate when you are away from home.

This mentality does mean you will have more work to make sure you have a consistent approach to interacting with your dog and your puppy. Any rules that apply to your dog must apply to the puppy, even if your puppy does not like it. Your Havanese is going to want to be in your lap or right next to you all of the time, something that may make your dog jealous, especially if you have a policy of no dogs on the furniture. If you break this rule with the puppy, you are going to have to let your dog on the furniture too. You cannot apply different rules. This is true even if you plan to enact the no dogs on the furniture rule once the puppy grows up. Odds are you won't. Since the Havanese does not get much bigger and the proportion of eyes to body remains pretty much the same, you are going to find it just as difficult to say no later. Having already trained the puppy that it is ok, you cannot change the rules later.

Avoid problems between the puppy and your dog by making the same rules for both dogs.

# Biting, Fighting, and Puppy Anger Management

One of the reasons that people do not want to start with a puppy is because of how challenging they can be. Havanese are typically even tempered and adorable, but as puppies they are also bursting with energy and do not know the rules. This means that they are going to be much more boisterous and potentially a danger to themselves or others. Even a laidback puppy can instigate a fight when riled up, and that energy can really get on a dog's nerves (particularly older dogs). There will be times when even your Havanese is unhappy, and this may result in tantrums and lashing out at your dog. It isn't common, but that doesn't mean it won't happen.

An untrained Havanese will take on the personality of the stereotypical small dog monster. To avoid this, you really have to start training your puppy early. Aggression isn't often a problem, but training can make sure that aggression isn't something your puppy adopts because there is nothing teaching the puppy not to behave in that way. If you see your Havanese starting to be aggressive (not just playing), immediately step in and let the puppy know that is not acceptable.

# Raising Multiple Puppies at Once

Only the bravest puppy parents adopt more than one puppy at a time, and this is true even with dogs like the Havanese. It is at least twice as much work, and you have to split your attention between two or more puppies at the same time. If you want to raise more than one Havanese puppy at once, you are in for a real challenge. They are going to want to please you and spend time with you, but they are also likely to feel something similar for each other. They have the same energy level and desire to learn, which means that their misbehaviors can feed off each other. It will take a lot more energy and work to make sure they behave the way you want them to act.

Be prepared to lose your personal life, particularly your social life, if you have more than one puppy at a time. Taking care of those little puppies is going to be like two full-time jobs at once. It is necessary to put a lot of work into training your puppies so that your home isn't destroyed twice as fast.

First, you must spend time with them, both together and separately. This means spending twice as much time with the puppies, making sure they get along well, learn at an even pace, and still get to have designated one-on-one time with you. Each puppy will have their own strengths and weaknesses, and you need to learn what they are for each one, as well as learn how well the puppies work together. If they both behave during alone time with you but tend to misbehave or fail to listen when they are together, you will need to adjust your approach to make sure they both understand the rules. This is a real challenge, especially if they whine when you are playing with one of them and not the other (which is very likely with Havanese).

You can always have someone else play or train with one puppy while you do the same with the other, then switch puppies. This builds bonds while letting the puppies know that they both have to listen to you and your training partner. Both puppies will also be happily occupied, so they won't be whimpering or feeling lonely while you are playing with the other one.

There may be some fighting between the puppies, and this is likely to start between three and six months of age. They don't tend to be as aggressive as other dogs, but it is still almost certain that there will be minor fights. This is fine as long as they are not too aggressive. Likely it won't be because Havanese are less concerned with where they are in the hierarchy than in being with their people. As long as they understand the rules and abide by them, fighting should not be a significant problem with your puppies.

During training, you will need to minimize distractions, both for your puppy and yourself. This is why serious training should be done one-on-one more often than together. Puppies are always watching and learning, especially a dog that is as enamored with you as the Havanese tends to be. If you do not properly train them, it will be your fault when they become difficult adults who won't listen to you. Be consistent and focused during training to avoid the worst behavior problems.

Photo Courtesy of
Susan Mahar

# CHAPTER 12
# Training Your Havanese Puppy

*"They are both intelligent and eager to please. They can learn tricks in a matter of minutes and were used in the old days as circus dogs for that reason."*

**Carol King**
*KingsKids Havanese*

Havanese are able to figure things out much faster than most small dogs and even a large percentage of the canine realm. Despite a ton of energy, training is far easier with a Havanese puppy than with most breeds. You aren't going to have to work through the kind of headstrong nature of many working dogs, and your Havanese is going to start to understand what you are trying to communicate relatively quickly in order to please you.

Still, working with a smart, energetic puppy can be tiring. By making sure to follow through with a few actions, you will find that your Havanese will pick up on the training much quicker. Keep in mind that training your puppy is a long-term commitment. Even if your Havanese isn't rebellious, the puppy is intelligent and will look for easier ways to do things. Your puppy won't want to anger you, but gentle begging and puppy eyes can be very effective, and they will learn that if you give in during a training session.

## Firm and Consistent

There are many times in life where you will feel something is close enough. This is never a good idea with intelligent dogs. They study their people and figure out ways to get what they want with as little work as possible. Wanting to please you will still drive a Havanese, but if you are willing to give an inch, they will take it and see how much further you can be pushed. Exceptions and leniency are seen by your puppy as having some control over the situation, and that is not what you want them to learn when they are young. It just makes it that much harder to make them take you seriously later.

Keeping a consistent and firm approach during training will make life for easier for you and your puppy. Even if you are tired at the end of a long day at work, you have to enforce the rules. No matter how cute or friendly your puppy is being, you must make sure that all of the rules you have been teaching remain firmly in place. If you don't feel up to it, have a family member do the training. If you don't have anyone to help you, you can change up the training a bit to make it more enjoyable. It is fine to change things up if you are having a rough time, as long as you remain consistent. Interacting with your Havanese can make for a much more enjoyable experience and can even cheer you up. Consistency and firmness do not mean that you have to do the same activities all of the time. You just need to make sure that your puppy understands that you are in charge and there is no negotiating on that. This will keep your puppy on the right track to be a great companion instead of a little dictator.

Photo Courtesy of
Sara Mullen

# Gain Respect Early

Being firm and consistent in your approach to training will start gaining you respect from your little canine early in your relationship. This is something you will need to keep building over time. Without respect, your Havanese is going to think you don't mean what you say and will start to try to get its own way. As long as you are firm and consistent, respect should be a natural part of the bond. That does mean that you cannot multi-task while you are training your puppy, or even just playing with your puppy. The Havanese wants your full attention and will find a way to get it, even if it means breaking the rules to get your attention.

Positive interaction is the best way to gain respect. Playing and training your puppy every day helps build a healthy, positive relationship that will teach your puppy where they fit into the pack. Your puppy learns that it is part of the family, but that you are the one in charge.

# Operant Conditioning Basics

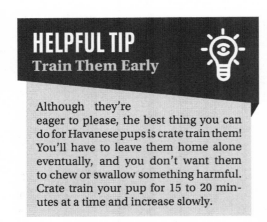

**HELPFUL TIP**
**Train Them Early**

Although they're eager to please, the best thing you can do for Havanese pups is crate train them! You'll have to leave them home alone eventually, and you don't want them to chew or swallow something harmful. Crate train your pup for 15 to 20 minutes at a time and increase slowly.

Operant conditioning is the scientific term for actions and consequences. What you have to do is provide your Havanese puppy with the right consequences for each behavior.

The best way to use operant conditioning is through positive reinforcement, particularly since the Havanese are so attached to people. This type of training is more effective with working dogs and dogs that have a long history with people because they want to please their people. They want to work with you and fulfill their tasks. Knowing that they are doing something right encourages their behavior a lot more than knowing when they do something wrong. With so much energy, they will be able to keep trying until they get it right.

There are two types of reinforcements for conditioning that you will be using in training your Havanese:

- Primary reinforcements (Operant Conditioning)
- Secondary reinforcements (Classic Conditioning)

# Primary Reinforcements

A primary reinforcement gives your dog something that it needs to survive, like food or social interaction. Both of these can be effective for Havanese – they love spending time with you and having treats. That is exactly what makes them so effective during training.

Initially, you will rely on primary reinforcements since you do not have to teach your Havanese to enjoy them. However, you have to keep a balance. Meals and play time should never be denied to your puppy, no matter how poorly the puppy performs. These things are essential to living, and you will have to give them – that is non-negotiable. It is things like treats and extra play time that you use to reinforce good behavior.

Err on providing too much attention and affection over too many treats. Because of their small stature, Havanese need to keep a well-balanced diet to remain healthy. If you rely on treats instead of attention, you are setting yourself and your pup up for serious problems later.

# Secondary Reinforcements

You use repetition to get good at your hobbies, sports, and other physical activities – this is secondary reinforcement. Without a doubt, Pavlov's experiment with dogs is the most recognizable example of secondary reinforcement. Using the bell, Pavlov taught the dogs that when the bell rang it meant it was time to eat. The test dogs began to associate the ringing of a bell to meal time. They were conditioned to associate something with a primary reinforcement (food). You can see this in your home when you use a can opener. If you have any cats or dogs, they probably come running as soon as the can opener starts going.

Secondary reinforcements work because your Havanese will associate the trigger with something that is required. This makes your puppy more likely to do as you tell it to do. Dogs who are taught to sit using a treat only will automatically react by sitting down when you have a treat in your hand. They won't even wait for you to tell them to sit. They know that sitting means more food, so they automatically do it once you make that association. Of course, this is not the proper training because they need to learn to sit when you say sit, and not when you have a treat. That is the real challenge.

Fortunately, it is relatively easy to train Havanese puppies with the right trigger because they are both intelligent and eager to please. While they may enjoy food, you can show them that the trigger is the word, not the food. They will get it much faster than many other dog breeds.

You can also use toys and attention as a way of getting your Havanese to do the right thing. If you have a regular schedule and you are willing to change it a little to give your puppy a little extra attention for doing something right, that will be just as effective as a treat because they love attention. You can take the pup on an extra walk, spend a little more time playing with a favorite toy, or take some time to cuddle with the puppy.

Sometimes punishment is required too, but you need to be very careful about how you do it. Trying to punish a Havanese can be tricky; however, denying your Havanese attention can work very well. Simply put your puppy in a penned off area where the Havanese can see you but cannot interact with you. The little guy will whine and whimper to let you know that he or she wants out. Don't give in because this is the punishment. Just ignore your puppy to teach the lesson about proper behavior.

Punishments must happen during the event. If your Havanese chews something up and you don't find out for several hours, it is too late to punish the puppy. The same is true for rewards. To reinforce behavior, the reward or punishment must be almost immediate. When you praise or punish your puppy, make sure you keep eye contact. You can also gently take the puppy by the scruff of the neck to ensure that you keep eye contact. You won't need to do that when you are praising your pooch because they will automatically keep eye contact. Havanese can be absolutely driven by hearing your praise.

Photo Courtesy of
Crystal Singleton

# Why Food Is A Bad Reinforcement Tool

The small Havanese stature means that food is not something you should use often. It does not take much for a Havanese to gain excess weight. With affection and attention being such successful motivators, it is best to use them as much as possible instead of getting your Havanese accustomed to treats for rewards. Use treats sparingly.

Photo Courtesy of Ava Brown

Another reason to use treats sparingly is because you don't want your puppy to respond to you primarily when you have food. If your Havanese associates training with treats, you may have a difficult time training your Havanese to listen to you without them.

Treats can be used in the early stages when your puppy's metabolism is high and has not been conditioned to respond to secondary reinforcement. This will give you something to help your puppy learn to focus as you train the puppy to understand other incentives. It should not take too long before you can start transitioning away from treats as a reinforcement tool. Treats are also the best way of training certain types of behavior, such as rolling over. Your puppy will automatically follow the treat, making it easy to understand what you mean.

Treats are also best for the beginning commands (Sit, Stay, and Leave it). Your dog does not understand words yet and will quickly make the connection between what you are saying and why the treat is being offered. Leave it is very difficult to teach without treats because there is no incentive to drop something if your puppy really wants the object that's already in their mouth. Treats are something that will make the puppy drop whatever is in the puppy's mouth as their attention and desire re-focus on the food.

# Small Steps to Success

The first few weeks, maybe even the first couple of months, are a time with a very steep learning curve. Your puppy is not going to understand what you are doing in the beginning as you try to convince your little Havanese to use the bathroom outside. The best way to train the puppy is to realize that you need to start slow – don't begin with expectations that your puppy will be housetrained within a week (that won't happen). Your puppy must learn the daily routine (which you will be doing at the same time). Once the schedule and environment are less exciting, your Havanese will have an easier time focusing during training sessions.

Training should begin from Day One. Even though your puppy is just getting to know the environment, you need to start putting some of the rules in place. As your puppy gets familiar with the world, you can teach the Havanese about its area and that the crate is for sleeping. Learning to go into the crate on command has some obvious benefits, particularly if you leave home every day. This is when you start using treats to train the puppy to go into the crate and do other basic activities.

Starting from Day One does not mean trying to do everything – you must start small. Give treats for little things that your puppy might do anyway, like explore the crate. Once your Havanese starts to understand the reward system, training will become easier.

# Why Trainers Aren't Always Necessary

Havanese really aren't dogs that require trainers because they are more than happy to listen to their people. Even if you want to train your Havanese to do more complicated tricks, you probably don't need a trainer, unless you are a complete novice with teaching puppies. Then the training is really more for you than for the puppy.

Havanese have been lap dogs for centuries, but unlike a lot of small dogs, they have enjoyed interacting with people and playing instead of just being lazy. They have energy and want to put it to good use. Watching them bounce around can be very therapeutic at the end of the day, which can make it as much of a way for you to unwind as it is a way for your puppy to learn.

If you have older dogs, they can be a great way of keeping your Havanese in check when you are gone – after your Havanese has been in the home for a couple of months. You will need to use the crate in the beginning, but with time, your older dog can be a great role model for how to spend the day in your absence. In the beginning, your absence should be very short, like going to get the mail. Then you can progress to slightly longer activities that take you out of the house for half an hour or so. With an older dog in charge, this can help your Havanese be more comfortable without you around the home.

If you don't have much time once the basics are done, you should consider getting a trainer to make sure your puppy doesn't forget them (though you are not off the hook). Since your Havanese will more likely react quicker to your training, it is well worth making sure you always have time for your puppy because no trainer is going to be as influential as you – your puppy loves you, not some stranger.

Photo Courtesy of
Terry Russo

# CHAPTER 13
# Basic Commands

There are so many tricks that your adorable Havanese puppy can learn, from fetch to wonderful feats of agility. All of that begins by training with a few simple commands. With these commands, your puppy will learn to not only do the most basic and necessary tricks, but will also learn how to learn. Once your puppy has these commands down, there will be a world of tricks that you can teach your cute little canine.

## Why Size and Personality Make Them Ideal Companions

Photo Courtesy of
Gino Piunno

Training is something that is a lot of fun with a Havanese dog. They are incredibly intelligent, and training them makes them even more fun to spend time with. When properly trained, they can be one of the best companions because they can travel with you anywhere you go. If a Havanese is well-trained, the people around you will also enjoy having the dog around too because the Havanese are famous for their fun and energy. They tend to love everyone and want to play. Since they can go with you virtually anywhere, training will quickly pay off as you and your best friend share some of the most memorable lessons. If your Havanese is not trained, it will be much harder to take your canine places as your Havanese will be wary of strangers and may bark far more than is comfortable for anyone around them.

# Picking the Right Reward

One of the most interesting aspects of having a Havanese is determining the right reward. You want to keep the treats to a minimum but that should be fine with a Havanese since there are so many other things that can motivate them. Treats may be a good starting point, but you will need to quickly switch to something that is a secondary reinforcer. Praise, additional play time, and extra petting are all fantastic rewards for Havanese pets since they care about how you feel and your reaction to them. Plopping down to watch a movie and letting the puppy sit with you will be a great reward after an intense training session. Not only did your puppy learn, but you both now get to relax and enjoy just chilling together.

If you begin to gain the respect of your Havanese, that can be used to help train your dog. At the end of each session, give your puppy extra attention or a nice walk to demonstrate how pleased you are with the progress that has been made.

# Successful Training

Training is about learning the commands. If your Havanese learns to respond only to the rewards (such as the dog that sits as soon as you have a treat in your hand), the training was not successful.

Gaining the respect of your dog is generally the key in being a successful trainer, but with Havanese it also means dedicated attention – you have all of the puppy's attention during a training session. As you and your Havanese work together, your dog will come to respect you (so long as you remain consistent and firm). Do not expect respect in the early days of training because your puppy does not have the understanding or relationship required to be able to understand. Fortunately, their intelligence will start to show early on, making it easy to see when they are starting to respond to you instead of just the reward. This is the time when you can start switching to rewards that are fun instead of those that center around food.

Even in the beginning, you need to make handling and petting a part of the reward. Although your dog does not quite understand it for what it is, your Havanese will begin to understand that treats and petting are both types of rewards. This will make it easier to switch from treats to a more attention-based reward system. Associating handling and petting as being enjoyable will also encourage your puppy to look at play time as a great reward. No matter how much they love to eat, being entertained and playing with you will be a welcome reward since it means the puppy is not alone or bored.

# Basic Commands

Photo Courtesy of Jenny Prieto

For the Havanese, there are five basic commands that you must teach them, and one that you will probably want to start training your puppy to understand. These commands are the basis for a happy and enjoyable relationship as your Havanese learns how to behave. By the time your puppy learns the five commands, the purpose of training will be clear to your Havanese. That will make it much easier to train them on the more complex concepts.

You should train the puppy in the order of the list as well. Sit is a basic command, and something all dogs as well as your Havanese already do. Teaching Leave it and how to bark less are both difficult and fight the instincts and desires of your Havanese pooch. They are going to take longer to learn than the other commands, so you want to have the necessary tools already in place to increase your odds of success.

Here are some basic guidelines to follow during training.

● Everyone in the home should be a part of the Havanese training because the Havanese needs to learn to listen to everyone in the household, not just one or two people.

● To get started, select an area where you and your puppy have no distractions, including noise. Leave your phone and other devices out of range so that you keep your attention on the puppy.

● Stay happy and excited about the training. Your puppy will pick up on your enthusiasm and will focus better because of it.

● Start to teach Sit when your puppy is around eight weeks old.

● Be consistent and firm as you teach.

● Bring a special treat to the first few training sessions, such as chicken or cheese.

Once you are prepared, you can get started working and bonding with your cute little Havanese.

## Sit

Once you settle into your quiet training location with the special treat, begin the training. It is relatively easy to train your dog to obey this command. Wait until your puppy starts to sit down and say Sit. If your puppy finishes sitting down, start to give praise for it. Naturally, this will make your puppy incredibly excited and wiggly, so it may take a bit of time before they will want to sit again. When the time comes and the puppy starts to sit again, repeat the process.

**HELPFUL TIP**
**Obedience = Safety**

*"Sit"* and *"stay"* are the basic commands that every dog should know, but it is particularly important that your Havanese receive this training as it may struggle with boundaries. Being that Havanese love attention, you can expect your pup to jump and paw at your legs. While it might be cute in the beginning, your house guests probably won't like it later on.

It is going to take more than a couple of sessions for the puppy to fully connect your words with the actions. In fact, it could take a little over a week for your puppy to get it. Havanese are intelligent, but at this age there is still so much to learn that the puppy will have a hard time focusing. Commands are something completely new to your little companion. However, once your puppy understands your intention and masters Sit, the other commands will likely be a little bit easier to teach.

Once your puppy has demonstrated a mastery over Sit, it is time to start teaching Down.

## Down

Repeat the same process to teach this command as you did for Sit. Wait until the puppy starts to lie down, then say the word. If the Havanese finishes the action, offer your chosen reward.

It will probably take a little less time to teach this command after you start training it.

Wait until your puppy has mastered Down before moving on to Stay.

## Stay

This command is going to be more difficult since it isn't something that your puppy does naturally. Be prepared for it to take a bit longer to train on this one. It is also important that your dog has mastered and will consistently sit and lie down on command before you start to teach Stay.

Choose which of these two commands you want to use to get started, then you will need to be consistent. Once your dog understands Stay for either Sit or Down, you can train with the second command. Just make sure the first position is mastered before trying the second.

Tell your puppy to either Sit or Stay. As you do this, place your hand in front of the puppy's face. Wait until the puppy stops trying to lick your hand before you begin again.

When the puppy settles down, take a step away from the Havanese. If your puppy is not moving, say Stay and give the puppy the treat and some praise for staying.

Giving the reward to your puppy indicates that the command is over, but you also need to indicate that the command is complete. The puppy has to learn to stay until you say it is okay to leave the spot. Once you give the okay to move, do not give treats. Come should not be used as the okay word, as it is a command used for something else.

Repeat these steps, taking more steps further from the puppy after a successful command.

Once your puppy understands Stay when you move away, start training to Stay even if you are not moving. Extend the amount of time required for the puppy to stay in one spot so that he or she understands that Stay ends with the okay command.

When you feel that your puppy has Stay mastered, start to train the puppy to Come.

## Come

This is the last in the series of commands since you cannot teach this one until the puppy has learned the previous commands. The other two commands do not require the puppy to know other commands to get started (it is just easier to train if the puppy already has an understanding of what commands are and how the puppy is expected to react to them).

Before you start, decide if you want to use come or come here for the command. You will need to be consistent in the words you use, so make sure you plan it so that you will intentionally use the right command every time.

Leash the puppy.

Tell the puppy to Stay. Move away from the puppy.

*Photo Courtesy of
Cortney Stauffer*

Say the command you will use for Come and give a gently tug on the leash toward you. As long as you did not use the term to indicate that the Stay command was done, your puppy will begin to understand the purpose of your new command. If you used the term to indicate the end of stay, it will confuse your puppy because the Havanese will associate the command with being able to move freely.

Repeat these steps, building a larger distance between you and the puppy. Once the puppy seems to get it, remove the leash and start at a close distance. If your puppy does not seem to understand the command, give some visual clues about what you want. For example, you can pat your leg or snap your fingers. As soon as your puppy comes running over to you, offer a reward.

## Leave It

This is going to be one of the most difficult commands you will teach your puppy because it goes against both your puppy's instincts and interests. Your puppy wants to keep whatever it is they have, so you are going to have to offer something better. It is essential to teach it early though, as your Havanese is going to be very destructive in the early days. You want to get the trigger in place to convince the puppy to drop things.

You may need to start teaching this command outside of the training arena as it has a different starting point.

Start when you have time to dedicate yourself to the lesson. You have to wait until the puppy has something in their mouth to drop. Toys are usually best. Offer the puppy a special treat. As the Havanese drops the toy, say Leave it, and hand over the treat.

This is going to be one of those rare times when you must use a treat because your puppy needs something better to convince them to drop the toy. For now, your puppy needs that incentive, something more tempting than what they have before your puppy can learn the command.

This will be one of the two commands that will take the longest to teach (Quiet being the other). Be prepared to be patient with your pup. Once your puppy gets it, start to teach Leave it with food. This is incredibly important to do because it could save your pooch's life. They are likely to lunge at things that look like food when you are out for a walk, and being so low to the ground, they are probably going to see a lot of food-like things long before you do. This command gets them to drop whatever they are munching on before swallowing it.

## Quiet

In the beginning, you can also use treats sparingly to reinforce Quiet. If your puppy is barking for no apparent reason, tell the puppy Quiet and place a treat nearby. It is almost guaranteed that the dog will fall silent to sniff the treat, in which case, say Good dog or Good quiet. It won't take too long for your puppy to understand that Quiet means no barking. However, it may take a while for your puppy to learn to fight the urge to bark. Be patient with your puppy because it is difficult to stop doing something that you do naturally. How long did it take you to learn to get up early in the morning or to go to bed at a certain time? It is similar for a Havanese to learn not to bark.

# Where to Go From Here

These are all the basic commands that you are likely to need with your Havanese. However, if you want your Havanese to do tricks, there is a world of possibilities once your puppy has the basics down. These commands are the foundation of training, and the Havanese is capable of learning so much more. Just make sure that the tricks that you teach are not too stressful for your puppy. As your puppy grows into an adult, you can start teaching tricks that highlight your puppy's agility. Fetch and other interactive tricks will be ideal because your Havanese will want to do them.

*Photo Courtesy of Sharon Russo*

## CHAPTER 14
# Nutrition

*"Havanese can have a sensitivity to chicken, resulting in allergies and licking of the paws or lots of scratching. My suggestion is to always feed the highest quality food you can afford. And pick a protein that isn't chicken- salmon, beef, lamb etc."*

**Katie Say**
*MopTop Havanese*

Y ou have heard about the importance of nutrition your entire life, and you know that nutrition is just as important for your dog. Most people want to take good care of their dogs. However, it is just as easy to fall into the habit of offering food that is decidedly unhealthy for canines. From letting them have scraps from your plate to providing far too many treats, many pets end up getting too many calories for their activity levels. As your dog ages, this could become a serious issue for the canine's health. Ensuring your Havanese gets the right nutritional balance is critical for a long, happy life.

## Why a Healthy Diet Is Important

Though they have a considerable amount of energy, Havanese are a very small breed. Overfeeding them is incredibly easy because they do not need a whole lot of food before they reach their caloric needs for the day. Many of the tricks and activities can expend a good bit of energy, but that does not mean that they need a lot of food. If you have a very busy schedule, it will be entirely too easy to have substantial lapses in activities levels while you are home. Your Havanese is still going to expect the same amount of food, regardless of activity level. This means they are likely to start putting on weight, which will be detrimental to their health.

You need to not only be careful of how much you feed your Havanese during meal time, but how many treats you offer over the course of the day. All food needs to be accounted for when you consider both nutritional and caloric intake. With those tiny little bodies, you need to be

96

aware of roughly how many calories your dog eats a day. If you notice that your dog is putting on weight, you will be able to adjust how much food the Havanese eats each day or change food to something with more nutritional value.

# Commercial Food

Though it is convenient, commercial dog food is a very flawed product. There is nothing natural about those little bits of food you are feeding your dog, and ultimately, it is far less healthy than making your dog's meals. However, for most people it is the option that will be chosen because preparing every meal is an incredibly lengthy process. For some, there simply isn't enough time in the day to make every meal.

If you are part of the majority of puppy parents buying commercial food, make sure that you are buying the best that you can. Take the time to research each of your options, particularly the nutritional value of the food. Always account for your dog's small stature, energy levels, and age. Your puppy may not need puppy food for as long as other breeds (or even other Havanese), and dog food for seniors may not be the best option for your senior Havanese. To provide more nutrition, you can mix some food into the processed food. This can help supplement any nutrients, as well as being a healthy addition to an otherwise entirely processed meal. The addition of a little bit of home-cooked food with each meal will make your Havanese excited to eat.

# Preparing Your Food Naturally At Home

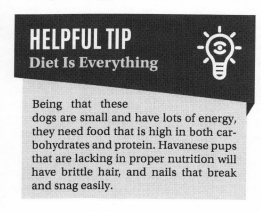

**HELPFUL TIP**
**Diet Is Everything**

Being that these dogs are small and have lots of energy, they need food that is high in both carbohydrates and protein. Havanese pups that are lacking in proper nutrition will have brittle hair, and nails that break and snag easily.

If you want to provide the healthiest meals possible, you should plan to spend an extra five to ten minutes in the kitchen per meal you prepare for your Havanese. If you regularly make your own food (from scratch, not with a microwave or boxed meal), it really isn't that much more time to provide an equally healthy meal for your little companion.

Keeping in mind the foods that your Havanese absolutely should not eat, you can mix some of the food you make for yourself into your Havanese's meal. Just make sure to add a bit more of what your Havanese needs to the puppy food bowl. Though you and your Havanese have distinctly different dietary needs, you can tailor your foods to include nutrients that your dog needs. It won't really take that much longer to tailor a meal for you and a slightly different version for your dog. Read through Chapter 5 to make sure that you never give your Havanese food that could be harmful or deadly.

Do not feed your Havanese from your plate. Split the food, placing your dog's meal into a bowl so that your canine understands that your food is just for you. The best home-cooked meals should be planned in advance so that your Havanese is getting the right nutritional balance.

Typically, 50% of your dog's food should be animal protein (fish, poultry, and organ meats). About 25% should be complex carbohydrates. The remaining 25% should be from fruits and vegetables, particularly things like pumpkin, apples, bananas, and green beans. These provide additional flavor that your Havanese will likely love while making the little pup feel fully faster so that overeating is less likely.

# Puppy Food Vs. People Food

It is true that puppies need more calories than adults, with their small size, Havanese puppies do not need nearly as much as you may think to meet caloric needs for their energy levels. If you are bringing a Havanese puppy into your home and know that you aren't going to have the time to cook, you should get food designed for puppies. This will ensure that your puppy gets the necessary calories for growth. Do not feed the puppy people food under the belief that you can switch to dog food later – because that is going to be virtually impossible by then. Once your Havanese becomes an adult, it is nearly impossible to convince your canine that those unappetizing pellets are food, particularly when your dog knows what the food on your plate tastes like. Do not set a precedence that will create significant problems for you later. If you feed your puppy home-made food, you are going to have to keep making food for your dog once the puppy stage is a memory.

It is best to make your puppy's food if you can. There really isn't going to be that much of a difference in amount of food between the puppy and adult stages. Their little bodies have special needs, and the first few months are critical. If you can make your puppy's meals (and know that you can keep it up when your Havanese is an adult), this will be a lot healthier for your dog.

If you find that you have to start buying commercial food, you will need to start slowly mixing it into your adult dog's meal. Do not be surprised if you find the pellets uneaten for a while. It will be a difficult process convincing your dog that is food, but if you mix it with other things (and know that you are always going to need to mix at least a little real food in with the commercial food), your dog will be more likely to start eating it since it will smell like the food.

Photo Courtesy of
Alyssa Pawlowski

# Dieting, Exercise, and Obesity

Your Havanese is not going to diet the way you may choose to diet. This means you have to keep a regular eating schedule for your dog – their day is going to be based largely on the times of the day that are designated to eating. If treats and snacks are something you establish as normal early on, your dog is going to believe that is also a part of the routine and will expect it. Obviously, this can be a terrible habit to establish with your Havanese, especially if it is food that you are sharing because you are snacking and feel guilty. You will need to make sure to be active after snacking so that your Havanese doesn't get too many calories. An extra round of play or another walk can go a long way to helping keep your Havanese at a healthy weight.

*Photo Courtesy of Judie Fahy*

There needs to be a healthy balance of diet and exercise to keep your Havanese from getting overweight, certainly to avoid your dog getting obese. Exercise is an absolute must. While you are helping your Havanese develop healthy eating and exercise habits, you are probably helping yourself. Being more aware of your dog's diet and exercise levels will also make you more aware of your own. Obesity is something that you will need to actively avoid with such a small dog. Get used to exercising and playing as a reward system.

## Warning About Overfeeding and the Right Caloric Requirement

You have to be careful of your Havanese weight, so you need to get used to monitoring it, particularly once your dog is an adult. Those snacks you share are not healthy, and your dog will pick up weight a lot faster than you will eating the same foods with less exercise. This is not really a reward for your Havanese – it's a hazard. Keep your dog on a diet that is healthy instead of indulging the little cutie. This will keep you both a lot happier in the long run.

Weighing your Havanese will be incredibly helpful to ensuring that the pooch is staying at a healthy weight. Because they are really toy-sized, you can use your own scale to weigh them. Gently pick up your canine and step on the scale. Subtract your weight from the total, and that is how much your Havanese weighs. Be honest about your weight. That does mean weighing yourself just before weighing your Havanese and being accurate with the number. Counting calories is incredibly time consuming, but you should also know roughly how many calories your Havanese eats in a day because it really does not take much to meet the needs of such a small dog.

# CHAPTER 15
# Grooming – Productive Bonding

*"Think of grooming as an opportunity to bond and build trust between you and your Havanese puppy. Always use a gentle tone of voice and a gentle hand when combing. Take it slow and soon your puppy will be looking forward to grooming time."*

**Veronica Guillet**
*Renaissance Havanese*

Havanese have a lovely coat of hair, not fur, and that is often a big draw. Since they are hypoallergenic, they are a popular choice for people with allergies who want dogs. However, it can be more time consuming to take care of a long coat of hair than a short coat of fur. On the plus side, you have a lot more potential if you want a dog that you can style. Your dog will look great with a long or short coat, so you can change up your pup's look based on the time of year.

Your Havanese will likely enjoy whatever time you spend during grooming because it is dedicated time with you. This is prime bonding time, just be careful when you work knots and other tangles out of your dog's hair. Enjoy the time you get to spend petting and interacting with your dog – you know the Havanese is enjoying it.

There are a few other grooming tips you should know to properly tend to your Havanese. Those large eyes will need some extra attention, and you will want to keep from getting the eyes and ears wet during bath time. This can be a real challenge with puppies, so be prepared.

## Managing Your Havanese Coat

Weekly or even daily brushing is the perfect way to bond with your puppy and to keep the relationship strong well into your Havanese's golden years. The regular attention will be something that your dog will look forward to as part of their routine. It will also be a nice way to relieve stress for you, as petting a dog is an easy way to help you calm down. Since they are quite small, it isn't going to be the chore that managing a large dog will be (although it is decidedly more time consuming than most small dogs if you keep your Havanese hair long).

## Puppy

As you can probably guess, brushing a puppy is going to take you more time. There will be a lot of wiggling and attempts at play. Trying to tell your puppy that the brush is not a toy clearly isn't going to work, so be prepared to be patient during each brushing session. On the other hand, they are so adorable, you probably won't mind that it takes a bit longer.

You can plan to brush your puppy after a vigorous exercise so that there is far less energy to fight or play. Be careful that you don't encourage rambunctious behavior during brushing because this will become part of the routine, and your Havanese will think that you enjoy it. Maybe you do in the beginning, but there will be times when you want to finish brushing your dog quickly, and that is why you need to make sure your puppy doesn't think it is time to play.

As you get accustomed to brushing your puppy, just get accustomed to checking their skin. Look for rashes, sores, or infections. You should also check their ears, ears, and mouth while you are grooming them. Keep doing these activities even after your Havanese is an adult. With such small bodies, it won't be that time consuming and will help you spot potential issues as early as possible.

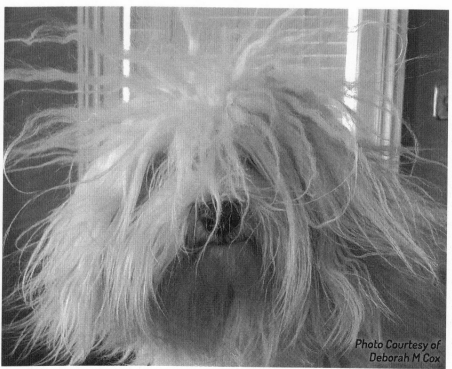

*Photo Courtesy of Deborah M Cox*

## Adulthood

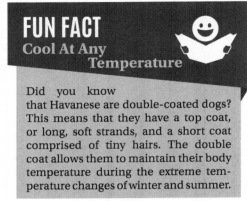

FUN FACT
Cool At Any Temperature

Did you know that Havanese are double-coated dogs? This means that they have a top coat, or long, soft strands, and a short coat comprised of tiny hairs. The double coat allows them to maintain their body temperature during the extreme temperature changes of winter and summer.

Brushing your dog daily will be best if you keep the dog's hair long. Even with short hair, it tangles a lot more easily and can quickly start to accumulate dirt and other items that can irritate your dog's skin. It won't be too much to make it nearly a daily activity. After all, they have hair, not fur. Just as you brush your hair every day, there are the same reasons to brush your Havanese's coat often. Make sure that the hair above your Havanese's eyes is kept short. It should never get in the dog's eyes. It would be best to have a professional take care of trimming your dog's hair on a regular basis.

Baths should be a regular part of the schedule too, though it will vary based on the time of year.

# Trimming the Nails

With small paws covered in hair, you have to be very careful about trimming your Havanese nails. If you feel at all uncomfortable, you might want to have a professional trim your Havanese nails. You can always learn how it is done and do it yourself over time. As a puppy though, your Havanese may be a little too rambunctious for you to do the cutting.

The puppy's nails should be cut about once a week since your Havanese will probably be on concrete and asphalt less often than a larger dog. Without these materials to help keep the nails filed, regular grooming will be required to keep the nails from being too long.

Once your dog is an adult, check the nails monthly. As you will be walking them more on surfaces that will help keep their nails shorter, trimming can be done less frequently. It is possible that you won't need to trim them for months at a time if your Havanese walks on concrete or asphalt enough to keep them short. However, if you don't walk as much on these surfaces in the winter, you will need to increase how often you trim the nails.

# Brushing Their Teeth

Havanese teeth should be brushed at least once a week (twice or three times is recommended). Considering they will be all over you, you will have a pretty good idea when to brush – if you can't stand the smell emanating from your dog's mouth, stop what you are doing and brush those teeth. Regular brushing keep your dog's teeth clean and healthy. If you notice that plaque and tartar are building up quickly or that your dog's breath is smelling foul faster, you can increase how often you conduct the brushing ritual.

# Cleaning Their Eyes

You will need to take extra care of your Havanese's eyes. They frequently tear up, and this can discolor the fur around their eyes. Having a professional groomer keep the hair short around their eyes will help, but you will still need to keep the eyes clean in between professional grooming sessions. Wiping their eyes daily with a damp cloth will help keep the staining to a minimum, as well as keep dirt from accumulating around the eyes. Do not apply pressure; gently wiping should be adequate.

# CHAPTER 16
# Preventative Health Treatments

Havanese make exceptionally fantastic companions, in large part due to their small stature and enthusiastic personalities. As long as you are careful and take good care of your little buddy, you will have a sweet little friend for a long time. They do get pretty excited, so they may not notice when they are injured; you should make sure never to be rough with your Havanese or that someone else is engaging in rough play with the dog.

In addition to making sure that your canine doesn't get too excited, there are some basic preventative measures you should take to make sure your puppy stays healthy. Many of the treatments and concerns are universal across the entire canine world, which means there is a good chance you already know that you need to take care of these things for your small dog. You can consider this chapter as more of a reminder or checklist of things you probably already know. Do make sure to add the treatments to your calendar and to your regular budget.

Photo Courtesy of
Audrey Just

# Fleas and Ticks

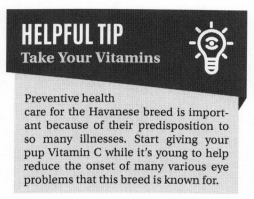

**HELPFUL TIP**

**Take Your Vitamins**

Preventive health care for the Havanese breed is important because of their predisposition to so many illnesses. Start giving your pup Vitamin C while it's young to help reduce the onset of many various eye problems that this breed is known for.

Havanese love to be with you, so if you don't spend a lot of time outdoors, they run a lower risk than many of the other breeds that love to be outside. However, your little Havanese is going to be outside some of the time, which means you still have to be worried about fleas and ticks. If your puppy loves roaming through high grass, you cannot allow any lapse in treatment, even in winter.

With each of the frequent baths that you give your Havanese, you should also check for ticks and fleas as part of the cleaning process. Comb through the hair and check the skin for irritation or parasites. This will help keep your puppy healthier and feeling much better. Since you will be doing this often, you should be able to know when a new bump appears. Since your dog will be very happy to spend time with you, it shouldn't take as long as you think – it isn't as though you will have to spend a lot of time struggling to get your Havanese to sit still for a tick check.

Fleas will be more problematic because they are far more mobile. The best way to look for fleas is to make it a regular part of your brushing sessions. You can also look for behavioral indicators, such as incessant scratching and licking. Check the spots where your dog is scratching to see if the skin is irritated or if it is the work of a flea. Given the small stature of your companion, fleas will have no trouble jumping on your Havanese from the grass or other vegetation. This means you will need to use flea preventative products on a regular basis.

If you want to use natural products instead of the chemical-filled products, set aside a few hours to research the alternatives and find out what works best for your Havanese. Do not increase the number of baths because their skin is sensitive and should not be over-washed, so don't make this part of the solution. Do verify that any natural purchases work before you buy them.

Remedies should be applied monthly. Establishing a regular schedule and adding it to the calendar will help you remember to treat your dog on schedule.

# Worms and Parasites

Although worms and other types of parasites are a less common problem than fleas and ticks, they can be more dangerous. There are a number of types of worms that you should be aware of:

- Heartworms
- Hookworms
- Roundworms
- Tapeworms
- Whipworms

One of the primary problems is that there isn't an easy to recognize set of symptoms to help identify when your dog has a problem with worms. However, you can keep an eye out of for these symptoms, and if your dog shows them, you should schedule a visit to the vet.

- If your Havanese is unexpectedly lethargic for at least a few days.
- Patches of fur begin to fall out (this will be noticeable if you brush your Havanese regularly) or if you notice patchy spaces in your dog's coat.
- If your dog's stomach becomes distended (expands), set up an appointment with your vet immediately to have them checked. Your dog's stomach will look like a potbelly.
- Your Havanese begins coughing, vomiting, has diarrhea, or has a loss in appetite.

These should be more obvious in a Havanese because they tend to be a higher energy dog, but they can also be very easy going. If you aren't sure, it is best to get to the vet as soon as possible to check.

If your dog has hookworms or roundworms, you will also need to visit a veterinarian to get checked. These worms can be spread to you from your dog through skin contact. If your dog has them, you are at risk of contracting them as well. Being treated at the same time can help stop the vicious cycle of continually switching which of you has worms.

Heartworms are a significant threat to your dog's health as they can be deadly. You should be actively treating your dog to ensure that this parasite does not have a home in your dog. There are medications that can ensure your Havanese does not get or have heartworms.

# Benefits Of Veterinarians

Your dog should have regular visits to your vet, just like you have regular checkups with your doctor. From regular shots to healthy physicals, vets will make sure that your Havanese stays healthy.

Since Havanese are such eager companions, you will have an easier time noticing when they are not acting quite themselves. Annual visits to the vet will ensure there isn't a problem that is slowly draining the energy or health from your dog.

Health checkups also make sure that your Havanese is aging well. If there are any early symptoms of something potentially wrong with your dog over the years (such as arthritis), you will be able to start making adjustments. The vet can help you come up with ways to manage pain and problems that come with the aging process. Your vet will be able to recommend adjustments to the schedule to accommodate your canine's aging body and diminishing abilities. This will ensure that you can keep having fun together without hurting your dog. These changes are well worth it in the end because your dog is able to keep enjoying time with you without suffering additional pain.

*Photo Courtesy of Tami Armstrong*

# Holistic Alternatives

Wanting to keep a dog from a lot of exposure to chemical treatments makes sense, and there are many good reasons why people are moving to more holistic methods. However, doing this does require a lot more research and monitoring to ensure that the methods are working – and more importantly, do not harm your dog. Unverified holistic medicines can be a waste of money, or worse, they can be harmful to your pet. Other methods have often been used for far longer, so there is more data to ensure that they aren't doing more harm than good. However, natural methods that work are always preferable to any chemical solution.

If you want to use a holistic medication, make sure to talk to your vet about your options. You can also seek out Havanese experts to see what they recommend before you start using any methods you are interested in trying. Read what scientists have said about the medicine. There is a chance that the products you buy from a store are actually better than some of the medications sold as being holistic.

Make sure you are thorough in your research and that you do not take any unnecessary risks with the health of your Havanese.

*Photo Courtesy of Barbara Knight*

# Vaccinating Your Havanese

Vaccination schedules are almost universal for all dog breeds, including Havanese. Use the following to ensure that your Havanese receives the necessary shots on time.

- The first shots are required between 6 and 8 weeks following the birth of your Havanese. You should find out from the breeder if these shots have been taken care of and get the records of them:
  - Corona virus
  - Distemper
  - Hepatitis
  - Leptospirosis
  - Parainfluenza
  - Parvo
- These same shots are required again at between 10 and 12 weeks of age.
- These same shots are required again between 14 and 15 weeks old, as well as his or her first rabies shot.
- Your dog will need to get these shots annually after that. Your Havanese will also need annual rabies shots afterwards.

If you plan to use your Havanese as a farm dog or other strenuous work, you will need to give your dog other shots. Consult with your vet to see what else your canine will need based on the kind of work he or she will be doing. Make sure to get the schedule for upkeep on these shots.

# CHAPTER 17
# **Health Concerns**

*"The Havanese remains a very healthy breed but, in my experience, the illnesses to watch for are Luxated Patella (dislocation of the knee cap), Legg~Perthes (disintegration of the hip bone), Chondrodysplasia (a growth disorder) and eye, thyroid and heart problems."*

***Julie Pollock***
*Highborn Havanese*

Having a pure-bred dog means that your canine has some known health issues that you will need to monitor for as they age. Knowing what the potential problems to watch for are can help you know what to do and when to talk to your vet. The sooner you start to counter any potential problems, the longer your Havanese is likely to live and the healthier they are likely to be. If you notice any of the symptoms listed in the earlier chapters, make sure to schedule an appointment with your vet to have your dog checked.

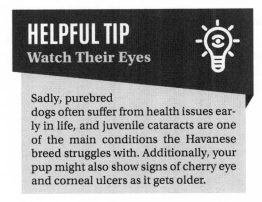

**HELPFUL TIP**
**Watch Their Eyes**

Sadly, purebred dogs often suffer from health issues early in life, and juvenile cataracts are one of the main conditions the Havanese breed struggles with. Additionally, your pup might also show signs of cherry eye and corneal ulcers as it gets older.

Adopting a puppy can give you the span of your dog's entire life to ensure they are as healthy as possible. The breeder should be able to provide health records in addition to any shot records and required tests. All of the details on the genetic and common ailments of Havanese are in Chapter 4. Making sure that the parents are healthy increases the likelihood that your puppy will remain healthy over his or her entire life. However, there is still a chance that your dog will have one of these problems even if the parents don't, so you will still need to keep an eye on your little friend.

*Photo Courtesy of
Ronda Flick*

# Typical Pure-Breed Health Issues

Fortunately, the Havanese are a very healthy breed, despite coming from just a few dogs that escaped from Cuba with their owners.

## Where You Can Go Wrong

While Havanese tend to be healthy, there are things that you can do that could damage your dog's health. These are related to the dog's diet and exercise levels. If you follow the recommendations in Chapter 14, your dog will remain healthy longer.

Photo Courtesy of
Kim Davis

## Importance Of Breeder to Ensuring Health in Your Havanese

Being aware of the health of the parents and the diseases that are known to be a problem for them will help you know what to monitor for in your Havanese.

Ask the breeder to talk about the history of the parents, the kinds of health problems that have been in the dog's family, and if the breeder has had problems with any particular illness in the past. If the breeder gives you only short or vague answers, this is a sign that you may be getting a Havanese that will have serious health problems later.

# Common Diseases and Conditions

The following are minor and occasional problems that some Havanese have:

● Patellar luxation
● PRA
● Otitis externa
● Cataracts

# Prevention & Monitoring

Beyond genetic issues (something you should learn about the parents before getting your puppy), the major problem you have to worry about is weight. The previous chapter provided a lot of details about how to ensure your puppy does not gain too much weight for their little frame. Considering the fact that they will eat whatever you give them, your dog's weight is always going to be a concern if you aren't careful. Your vet will likely talk to you if your dog has too much weight on its body because this not only puts a strain on the dog's legs, joints, and muscles, it can have adverse effects on your dog's heart, blood flow, and respiratory system.

## CHAPTER 18
# Your Aging Havanese

Havanese have an expected life-span of between 12 and 14 years, giving you more than a decade to train and enjoy your puppy's company. Havanese are considered to be seniors when they are 9 years old. As your dog ages, you will need to start making adjustments to accommodate his or her reduced abilities. A dog may remain healthy his or her entire life, but the body just won't be able to do the same activities at 12 that it could do at 2. The changes you need to make will be based on your Havanese's specific needs. The decline tends to be gradual, just little things here and there, like your Havanese having less traction on smooth surfaces. Over time, the body will start to deteriorate and your dog will not be able to jump as high.

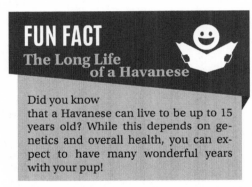

**FUN FACT**
**The Long Life of a Havanese**

Did you know that a Havanese can live to be up to 15 years old? While this depends on genetics and overall health, you can expect to have many wonderful years with your pup!

As your Havanese slows down, you need to make sure that he or she is not overdoing it. You should always make sure your dog doesn't over-exercise, but this is even more important for an older dog. Havanese will keep that happy demeanor and attitude, so it is up to you to monitor for any new limitations. These later years will be just as much fun, you will just need to make sure your Havanese isn't pushing beyond their limitations. It is easy to make the senior years incredibly enjoyable for your Havanese and yourself by making the necessary adjustments that allow your dog to keep being active without over exertion.

## Senior Dog Care

Your senior Havanese is going to be just as easy to care for as it is at any other point in your dog's life. Naps are just as enjoyable as walks. Sleeping beside you while you watch television or even if you nap with your dog is pretty much all it takes to make your Havanese happy.

However, you must continue to be vigilant about diet and exercise. Now is not the time to let your Havanese start eating anything and everything or neglect to take on regular walks. A senior Havanese cannot handle extra weight, so you must be careful to ensure he or she remains healthy with age.

If your canine cannot manage long walks, make the walks shorter and more numerous and spend more time romping around your yard or home.

When it comes to items that your Havanese will need to access regularly, you will need to make some changes to your current configuration.

- Set water bowls out in a couple of different places so that your dog can easily reach them as needed. If your Havanese has issues with his or her spine, you can place slightly raised water dishes around the home to make it easier for him or her to drink.

- Cover hard floor surfaces (such as tiles, hardwood, and vinyl). Use carpets or rugs that will not slip out from under your Havanese.

- Add cushions and softer bedding for your Havanese. This will both make the surface more comfortable and help your Havanese stay warmer. There are some bed warmers for dogs if your Havanese displays achy joints or muscles.

- Increase how often you brush your Havanese to improve his or her circulation. This should be very agreeable to your Havanese as a way to make up for other limitations that mean you can't do other activities as often.

- Stay inside during extreme heat and cold. Your Havanese is hardy, but the old canine body cannot handle the extreme changes as well as once it did.

- Use stairs or ramps for your Havanese instead of constantly picking up your canine. Picking your Havanese up may be more convenient for you, but it is not healthy for your Havanese. Let your dog maintain this bit of self-sufficiency.

- Avoid changing your furniture around, particularly if your Havanese shows signs of vision loss. A familiar home is more comforting and less stressful as your pet ages. If your Havanese is not able to see as clearly as he or she once did, keeping the home familiar will make it easier for your dog to move around without getting hurt.

- If you have stairs, consider setting up an area where your dog can stay without having to use the stairs as often.

- Create a space where your Havanese can relax with fewer distractions and noises. Your Havanese probably will not want to be alone often or for extended periods, but you should have a place where your older dog can just relax without loud or startling noises.

- Be prepared to let your dog out more often for restroom breaks.

# Nutrition

Since a decrease in exercise is inevitable for any aging dog, you will need to adjust your pet's diet. If you opt to feed your Havanese commercial dog food, make sure you change to senior food. If you make your Havanese's food, take the time to research how best to reduce calories without sacrificing taste. Your canine is going to need less fat in his or her food, so you may need to find something healthier that still has a lot of taste to supplement the types of foods you gave your Havanese as a puppy or active adult dog.

Photo Courtesy of Lise Kingsbury

# Exercise

Exercise will be entirely up to you because your Havanese is still just happy to be with you. If you make fewer demands, decrease the number of walks, or in any way change the routine, your Havanese will quickly adapt to the new program. It is up to you to adjust the schedule and keep your Havanese happily active. Usually increasing the number of walks with shorter durations will help keep your Havanese as active as necessary.

Keep in mind that your Havanese is more likely to gain weight in the later years, something that his or her body really cannot handle. Make sure that the activity is not reduced too much so that your canine does not become obese.

This will probably be the hardest part of watching your Havanese age. However, you will need to watch your Havanese for signs of tiredness or pain so that you can stop exercising before your dog has done too much. Your pace will need to be slower and your attention more on your dog, but ultimately it can be just as exciting. You will probably notice that your Havanese spends more time sniffing. This could be a sign that your dog is tiring, or it could be his or her way of acknowledging that long steady walks are a thing of the past and is stopping to enjoy the little things more. It is an interesting time and gives you a chance to get to understand your Havanese as the years start to show.

*Photo Courtesy of*
*Tami Armstrong*

# Mental Stimulation

Unlike the body, your Havanese's mind is likely going to be just as sharp and clever in the golden years. That means you can start making adjustments to focus more on the activities that are mentally stimulating. You can start doing training for fun because your Havanese will be just as able to learn now as when he or she was a puppy. Actually, it is likely to be easier because your Havanese has learned to focus better.

Your Havanese will be grateful for the shift in focus and additional attention. Getting your senior Havanese new toys is one way to help keep your dog's mind active if you do not want to train your dog or if you just don't have the time. You can then teach the Havanese different names for the toys because it will be fascinating (after all, he or she will still work for praise). Whatever toys you get, make sure they are not too rough on your dog's older jaw and teeth.

Hide and seek is another game that your aging Havanese can manage with relative ease. Whether you hide toys or yourself, this can be a game that keeps your Havanese guessing.

# Regular Vet Exams

Just as humans go to visit the doctor more often as they age, you are going to need to take your dog to see your vet with greater frequency. The vet can make sure that your Havanese is staying active without being too strained, and that there is no unnecessary stress on your older dog. If your canine has sustained an injury and hidden it from you, your vet is more likely to detect it.

Your vet can also make recommendations about activities and changes to your schedule based on your Havanese's physical abilities and any changes in personality. For example, if your Havanese is panting more now, it could be a sign of pain from stiffness. Your vet can help you determine the best way to keep your Havanese happy and active during the later years.

# Common Old-Age Aliments

Chapters 4 and 17 cover the illnesses that are common with a Havanese, but old age tends to bring a slew of ailments that are not particular to any one breed. Here are the things you will need to watch for (as well as talking to your vet about).

- Diabetes is probably the greatest concern for a breed that loves to eat as much as your Havanese does, especially with such a small frame. Though it is usually thought of as a genetic condition, any Havanese can become diabetic if not fed and exercised properly. It is another reason why it is so important to be careful with your Havanese's diet and exercise levels.

- Arthritis is probably the most common ailment in any dog breed, and the Havanese is no exception. If your dog is showing signs of stiffness and pain after normal activities, it is very likely that he or she has arthritis. Talk with your vet about safe ways to help minimize the pain and discomfort of this common joint ailment.

- Gum disease is a common issue in older dogs as well, and you should be just as vigilant about brushing teeth when your dog gets older as you do at any other age. A regular check on your Havanese's teeth and gums can help ensure this is not a problem.

- Loss of eyesight or blindness is relatively common in older dogs, just as it is in humans. Unlike humans, however, dogs don't do well with wearing glasses. Have your dog's vision checked at least once a year, and more often if it is obvious that his or her eyesight is failing.

- Kidney disease is a common problem in older dogs, and one that you should monitor for the older your Havanese gets. If your canine is drinking more often and having accidents regularly, this could be a sign of something more serious than just aging. If you notice this happening, get your Havanese to the vet as soon as possible and have him or her checked for kidney disease.

# Enjoying the Final Years

The last years of your Havanese's life can actually be just as enjoyable (if not more so) than earlier stages. The activities that the two of you used to do will be replaced with more attention and relaxation than at any other time. Finally having your Havanese be calm enough to just sit still and enjoy your company can be incredibly nice (just remember to keep up his or her activity levels instead of getting too complacent with your Havanese's new found love of resting and relaxing).

## Steps and Ramps

Havanese are small, but that does not mean that you should be picking them up more often as they age. Picking up your dog more often can even do even more physical harm. There are two good reasons to ensure your Havanese is able to move around on their own.

- An aging body means it is less safe and healthy to be picked up often.
- Independence in movement is best for you and your Havanese. You do not want your Havanese to come to expect you to pick him or her up every time he or she wants to get on the furniture or into the car.

Steps and ramps are the best way to ensure your Havanese is not too pampered (perhaps spoiled is a better word). It also keeps your dog's back from undergoing unnecessary stress.

## Enjoy the Advantages

A Havanese can be just as much fun in old age because his or her favorite thing is being with you. Your pet is still smart as can be, but has learned to chill a bit more.

Your little friend makes a fantastic therapy dog, so you can take them to places where therapy dogs are needed (particularly nursing homes). Since the Havanese don't shed, your dog isn't likely to cause problems among those you do visit. This can be a great way to relax or release frustration after a long or difficult day. An older Havanese is a fantastic companion to come home to because your little buddy wants nothing more than to be with you. As long as you are there, he or she is very happy. Sometimes that is all it takes to turn a disaster of a day into something bearable.

Your pet will find the warmest and most comfortable places, and will want you to join him or her.

Your dog is incredibly devoted and will be happy just to share a short stroll followed by a lazy evening at home.

## What to Expect

Your Havanese probably isn't going to suffer from fear that you are less interested in spending time together. He or she will continue to be the happy, friendly little dog you have always loved, which is why you have to be careful. Your canine's limitations should dictate interactions and activities. If you are busy, make sure you schedule time with your Havanese to do things that are within those limitations. Your happiness is still of utmost importance to your dog, so let the little canine know you feel the same way about his or her happiness. It is just as easy to make an older Havanese happy as it is with a young one, and it is easier on you since relaxing is more essential.

*Photo Courtesy of Kimberley Sample*

Made in the USA
Las Vegas, NV
08 April 2021